DESTINATION UNKNOWN

DESTINATION
UNKNOWN

ADVENTURES OF A LIFETIME SERIES

ZEV SPEKTOR

Destination Unknown
Adventures of a Lifetime Series ~ Book 1
© 2011 by Zev Spektor

ISBN: 978-1-60763-065-4

Editor: Miriam Jakubowicz
Proofreader: Hadassa Goldsmith
Cover artwork: Studio GFX
Cover design and internal layout: Justine Elliott

THE JUDAICA PRESS, INC.
123 Ditmas Avenue / Brooklyn, NY 11218
718-972-6200 / 800-972-6201
info@judaicapress.com
www.judaicapress.com

Manufactured in the United States of America

*The
One Above
has many
agents below.*

THANKS TO...

My wife for everything.

My in-laws for raising my wife.

My mother for always being there for us.

My children for being my best teachers.

Reb Nachum Shapiro for believing in this project.

Mrs. Miriam Jacubowicz for her editorial expertise.

Reb Yaakov Astor for the "spark," as well as the sound advice.

And others too numerous to mention ...

CHAPTER ONE

When Rebbe Yitzchak asked me to come along with him on a mission, I could hardly believe my ears. I was only twelve years old, and I was definitely not the most diligent student in the yeshivah of the small town outside of Yerushalayim where I lived. Besides, Rebbe Yitzchak was one of the greatest *chachamim* of the time. He'd written many well-known *sefarim* on all areas of Torah, including the hidden parts.

Rebbe Yitzchak had gone on several missions to oversee the collection of funds for the communities of Eretz Yisrael. He'd recently returned from one of these journeys, so it was a little strange that he was going on another one so soon — but who was I to ask questions? If Rebbe Yitzchak decided to go on another mission, that was his business, not mine.

But when he asked me, Avraham Siman, to come along with him — *that* was my business.

I can still remember our conversation.

"Avraham, how are things with you?"

"Well, I'm worried about my father, Rebbe."

Rebbe Yitzchak knew my story. "I can understand that, Avraham," he said. "And how is your mother holding up?"

"She acts bravely to encourage my sisters and me, but inside I'm sure she's as worried as I am."

Rebbe Yitzchak was silent for a moment. "Avraham," he finally said, "I will be leaving Eretz Yisrael again shortly on another journey."

I didn't know why Rebbe Yitzchak felt it necessary to tell me this, and I wasn't sure what to say.

"I want you to accompany me, Avraham."

"Me?" I repeated, dumbfounded.

"Yes, Avraham. You."

"I ..."

"Well?"

"I mean, Rebbe understands that with my father away, it might not be the best time."

"I understand, and nevertheless I want you to accompany me."

"I have to ask my mother."

"Fair enough, Avraham. Bring me your answer as soon as you can."

I wondered why Rebbe Yitzchak was asking me rather than my mother, but then again, Rebbe Yitzchak has his ways.

Although I was thrilled that Rebbe Yitzchak had asked

me to come along, I didn't feel like I could go. How could I leave my mother and sisters on their own? My father, Rebbe Daniel, a great *talmid chacham* and disciple of the revered *mekubal* Rebbe Suleiman, *zichrono livrachah*, and one of a long line of *rabbanim*, had disappeared nearly a month ago. Either he'd left for some reason, or … or who knew what happened to him?

I felt awful when I wondered what had become of my father. I sometimes lay awake at night thinking about him. I even cried myself to sleep, although of course, I never admitted to it. So when I told my mother about Rebbe Yitzchak's request and she insisted that I go, I was flabbergasted.

"But I can't leave you and Tziporah and Sarah alone," I protested.

"You're not leaving us alone. Remember what Abba always teaches us about Hashem being so close? And He has his messengers here in town who will look out for us."

I could barely contain my excitement.

When I told Rebbe Yitzchak that my mother had agreed to the trip, he didn't seem very surprised. "You'd better get ready, Avraham. We'll be leaving soon."

"Yes, Rebbe. I will."

As I made preparations for the trip, I was busy thinking. I was excited to be going, as any boy my age would be. Who wouldn't want the adventure? This would be even more exciting than the summer I had spent at Uncle Gavriel's farm in the north. But deep down in my heart, I also had another reason for wanting to go.

Perhaps I would find my father. Maybe while on the streets of some strange foreign city, I would spot him. I would run over to him and he would explain where he'd been and why he'd gone away. I didn't mention this to a soul; it was my secret. It was a far-fetched hope, but hope can be as far fetched as you want it to be, can't it?

My mother insisted that I buy a new robe for the journey.

"You'll be visiting new places and seeing important people," she told me.

"So what, Ima?"

"So you must be properly dressed."

"Why?"

"Because you represent Eretz Yisrael, that's why."

My mother's tone left no room for argument. So with mixed emotions, I took the precious coins she gave me. On the one hand, it would be nice to get a new robe for traveling, but on the other hand, I was taking her money — money that was not easy for her to come by.

When I went to buy the robe, something upsetting happened. The man who sold robes was generally a fine person, but sometimes people can be insensitive. As he was fitting me, he asked, "Do you think this is the right time to be going on a trip?"

I said nothing.

"I mean, with your father gone and all that."

I knew what he meant. He needn't have explained himself.

"Don't you think your mother might need you?"

I continued to keep quiet. Didn't people think? Didn't he realize that I'd thought of that? Did he think my mother didn't know what was best for her and my sisters? Didn't he trust Rebbe Yitzchak's judgment? I felt bad, but I kept quiet.

My mother was very happy with the new robe I had purchased. "It makes you look very handsome," she exclaimed.

I shrugged.

"Your father would be proud," she said, and her eyes became teary. I didn't know what to say. Then she corrected herself, "Your father *will* be proud."

I fought with myself. Should I disclose my well-hidden secret, my secret hope? Finally, I just couldn't hold back. "Ima, maybe I'll find Abba," I blurted out.

She looked at me hard. "Maybe you will," she said.

Aside from being a housewife, my mother had a little business. Truthfully, it was more than a business; it was a beloved hobby. Actually, to her it was an *avodah*, a gift to Hashem.

My mother is a very talented artist, and she'd spend her spare time making small wooden paintings of objects of *kedushah* like *sifrei Torah*, *tefillin* and *batei kenesses*. It provided her with some extra income, but it meant much more to her than that.

After I showed her the robe, she went to the metal case where she kept her paintings. She reached in and pulled out one I had never seen before. It was a painting the size of my hand, depicting the holy Mikdash. I'm no art expert, but I thought it was the most amazing thing I'd ever seen. It looked so real.

"Here, Avraham, take it," my mother said, handing it to me.

"Why, Ima?"

"You don't want it?"

"I do, Ima, but why are you giving it to me?"

"I want you to have it for whenever you need it."

"Why now, Ima?"

"So you'll have it whenever you need it."

As with the robe, she said it in a way that left me no room to argue. I took it.

"It's very nice, Ima. I'll always treasure it."

"You'll do with it as you see fit," she said, and turned away. I knew she was about to cry, and to be honest, so was I.

(

The day before we left, I met my good — maybe my best — friend, Moshe.

"So, I hear you're leaving soon," he remarked.

Rebbe Yitzchak had told me to keep the exact day of our departure a secret, but apparently Moshe had heard that it was coming up.

"Yes."

"Rebbe Yitzchak is keeping this trip quiet, but leave it to your good friend Moshe to find out about it." He smiled. "Well, I'm really glad for you."

I knew he meant it. He must have been terribly disappointed that he wasn't chosen to go, but he was sincerely happy for me. Then he said something that had anyone else said it, I might have been offended. But when Moshe said it, it didn't bother me; maybe that's because I knew he meant it.

"I think that in your heart, Avraham, you hope to be able to find your father on this journey. I hope you do."

I said nothing. I didn't want my voice to betray my

emotions. Then Moshe took out a small cloth package from his robe. He handed it to me.

"What is it?" I asked.

"It's for your trip. You never know when it might come in handy."

I opened it and saw the little knife Moshe always carried with him. "No, I can't take —"

"Please, Avraham, I want you to have it for the trip. Who knows, you might need it to cut berries off a tree somewhere."

I laughed; I thought his comment was funny. But somewhere deep inside of me, I felt a faint feeling of dread. I wondered what I might *really* need the knife for. Would there be danger on this journey? Fiercely, I told myself to stop thinking that way. Why was I always so nervous?

If Moshe noticed the inner conversation I was having with myself, he didn't say anything. "You can give it back to me when you return" was all he said.

"I really appreciate this, Moshe."

"It's nothing," he said, waving his hand.

Moshe is a true friend. I knew that I would miss him, as well as everyone else in our town.

"*Tzeischem leshalom*, Avraham," he said, and we shook hands. Then I went on my way.

CHAPTER TWO

We set out by camel in a small caravan early the next morning. There were five of us: Rebbe Yitzchak, a *bachur* named Yaakov Agir, who was around my age, two hired Arab hands, and myself. One of the Arab men was known as Musa. It seemed to me that we would have to keep our eyes on Musa; something seemed strange about him. The other Arab was known as Ahmed. Ahmed couldn't speak; he communicated by using hand motions and making little sounds. He was pretty good at it, and he was able to make himself understood quite well.

When I met Yaakov, I knew things were not going to go smoothly between us. He came from a village in the north, and they do things a little differently there. That wasn't the real problem, though. He just wasn't friendly. I tried to get along with him, but he was like a turtle in a shell; you can knock, but if it doesn't want to come out, it doesn't. I might not have been the best student, but I'm good at understanding people, and I really felt that underneath the unfriendly exterior, Yaakov was probably a nice enough fellow. That didn't help me — or him — now, though, when he was so hard to get through to.

We were traveling along the Mediterranean coast to Aza, from where we would continue on to Alexandria. From Alexandria, we would board a ship to Italy.

Several hours after we began the journey, a choice between two paths came up. Ahmed motioned one way, and Musa the other. Without hesitation, Rebbe Yitzchak said, "Musa, I am sure your way will take us where we need to go, but I've been here before. We will go the other way; it's shorter."

Musa shrugged and simply answered, "Whatever the Rabbi says."

Rebbe Yitzchak amazed me. As we traveled, he seemed to be in a completely different world, totally lost in thought. Yet, he was also the most down-to-earth man I have ever met. On that first day, I was traveling a little to the side of the caravan, when I heard Rebbe Yitzchak calling me.

"Avraham, come quick or you will miss it," he said.

I moved my camel closer to his, and looked as he pointed toward a brilliant spot of purple foliage blooming in the midst of the sand. He thrust his hand upwards, and exclaimed, "How great are Your creations, Hashem!"

As we traveled, I considered how I felt about this journey. I was excited, that's for sure. Who wouldn't be? Yet my excitement was tempered with sadness and uncertainty. I wanted to know where my father was, and wondered how my mother and sisters would fare. Since my father had been gone, I'd been sort of taking his place, and I hoped my sisters would be able to watch out for my mother as *I* had since my father's disappearance. When I bade them farewell, I didn't even tell them to look out for Ima; they would have wondered why I was stating the obvious. They would have said, "Of course we will," and in truth, I was sure they really would.

In the weeks since my father had been gone, I'd thought about him often, but I never dreamed of him. That first night, though, when we slept under our tents on the desert sand, I dreamed of him. I saw him sitting at his table with a *gemara*. He wasn't facing me, and he was at a great distance, but it was clearly him. I called to him, but he didn't hear me. That's all I remember from the dream. But I'm getting ahead of myself in speaking of that first night, for something happened shortly before nightfall.

We had finished Minchah and gotten back on our camels, when Rebbe Yitzchak became very still. I began to ask what had happened, but he motioned for silence. "Hashem is One," he said. "There is no other."

No one said a word.

And then we heard the camels approaching. In the dwindling light, we could make out armed Arab men. At first there were two or three, then more appeared. The Arabs moved their camels to the side to let a man wearing a sheik's turban ride through. He did not look like a very nice fellow. He smiled — if you can call it that — and looked at Rebbe Yitzchak.

"Abu Rash at your service, Rabbi," he said, the smile turning into a sneer.

The name struck fear in my heart.

Recently reports had been reaching our town of the sheik known as Abu Rash. Abu Rash was known far and wide as the leader of one of the most ruthless and bloodthirsty criminal bands in the country. It was said that since he had no sons, he considered his criminal organization to be his son, and all of his energies were dedicated to running his illegal activities. Eretz Yisrael was under the rule of the Ottoman Empire, but as long as he did not interfere with government activities, the authorities of the Ottoman Empire in Turkey did not interfere with Abu Rash and his men, and they were free to do as they pleased. It would have been too much of an effort for the Ottomans to send the soldiers necessary to put down Abu Rash's band. So as long as they did not prove too much of a nuisance to the government, they were safe.

And now, for some reason, they had come to this area of the country. I had heard they were within a day's ride from Yerushalayim, and now I saw that this was indeed the case. Here, not ten yards in front of me, was the infamous man himself. I wondered if he had noticed that Rebbe Yitzchak was a *chacham* or if he actually recognized that he was face to face with a man of Rebbe Yitzchak's stature. I was not kept wondering for long.

"I have heard of you, Rabbi Yitzchak, but we have never met. Isn't that so?"

"I don't believe I have had the pleasure of meeting you until now, no," Rebbe Yitzchak said as if he was speaking to the new shoemaker in town. In his eyes I saw nothing but calm.

"My spies told me that you were coming this way, and they were correct."

"Yes, they were."

"To what do we owe the pleasure of your presence in these parts?"

"Surely, if you know of me, you know that I do much traveling."

"Yes, I know that."

"Well, there you have your answer."

"Not so fast, honorable Rabbi. I happen to know that you just returned from one of your charity missions."

"Yes."

"Do you always embark upon a journey so soon after returning?"

"Times are difficult, are they not?"

Abu Rash laughed. "Yes, you are right, Rabbi. Times are difficult, but then again aren't times always difficult?"

"If there is a need to oversee the collection of charity, what can I do?"

"Honored Rabbi," Abu Rash said as his hand gently touched the saber that hung at his side, "could I ask you to introduce me to the members of your party?"

Rebbe Yitzchak, who until now had been conversing with Abu Rash in a polite fashion, looked almost as if had lost patience with the man. He said nothing, but there was a distant look on his face.

"Rabbi, did you hear me?" Abu Rash was clearly not used to being ignored.

"Abu Rash," Rebbe Yitzchak said, addressing the bandit leader by name for the first time, "the time has come for us to move on, before dark descends."

There was confusion on Abu Rash's face; apparently,

people did not usually end conversations with him before he allowed them to do so. I looked at Rebbe Yitzchak, aware that I had probably never been in such danger. I was perhaps the closest to him, yet I could not really make out what he said next. Then he looked at me and said, "We go now." I didn't move. He looked at me and with great intensity said, "Go now, my son. You are safe."

You don't ignore something like that. I moved my camel forward. I could see the face of the man nearest Abu Rash; he was staring at me intently. I passed him as well as the other men and did not look back. From behind me, I could hear Rebbe Yitzchak urging the others to go as well.

In a few moments we were all together on the path. It was almost dark. Yaakov, his voice shaky, said, "They will come after us, they will find us …."

"They cannot" was all Rebbe Yitzchak said. We continued on in the darkness in utter silence.

Later I would ask Rebbe Yitzchak about this episode, but now we all traveled on, numb with relief.

"Hashem is One," said Rebbe Yitzchak. "There is no other."

CHAPTER THREE

The next morning, shortly after we resumed our journey, Rebbe Yitzchak motioned for me to come close to him. I brought my camel near his, and we rode together in silence for a few minutes.

"Avraham, I want to explain something to you about this mission we have undertaken."

I looked at Rebbe Yitzchak, wondering what he was going to say.

"You know, of course, that your father is not the first of his family to be the *chacham* in your town."

"Yes."

"He comes from a long line of *talmidei chachamim* who have been the spiritual leaders of the town."

I nodded.

"The leaders in the town and in fact the entire area have come from your family for many years, and probably will continue to come from your family for many years to come."

Now, had this been anyone else, I might have asked what the point of this was, but it wasn't anyone else. It was Rebbe Yitzchak. I must have betrayed my thoughts with my expression, though, because he smiled and said, "I know that I'm telling you nothing you don't already know."

I tried to deny that this was exactly what I'd been thinking, but Rebbe Yitzchak waved his hand and smiled again. "No, it's true. But there is a reason I'm reminding you of these things."

"Does it have to do with my father's disappearance?"

"Yes, Avraham, it does."

I sat forward so I wouldn't miss anything Rebbe Yitzchak said.

"You see, a little while back, it came to our attention that our friend Abu Rash wanted to spread his net over the area outside of Yerushalayim. He knew that if he tried to do so, your father, may he be well, would stand in his way. The welfare of that area has been the responsibility of your family for generations, and Abu Rash understood that your father would not let it fall under his control without a fight."

"What does this have to do with my father's disappearance?" I asked, fear rising inside of me.

"Well, Avraham, Abu Rash therefore decided that your father had to go."

"Go?"

"Well, if he felt that he could have simply pressured your father to permanently leave the area, I'm sure he would have

done that, so as not to rile up the Jewish population. He knew,
though, that your father would not be pressured. So we believe
that he decided that he must get rid of your father — forever."

I felt faint. "To kill him?"

"Yes, my son. Abu Rash signed a warrant for his men to
do your father in."

"Is he …?"

"I believe your father is fine. When we became aware
of the situation, we decided that your father must flee Eretz
Yisrael for the time being."

"Does Rebbe know where he is?"

"No, Avraham, I really do not — since we felt it would
be best if no one but he knew where he was headed — but
I have every reason to believe he is safe. He left before Abu
Rash moved his band anywhere near the area. With the help
of Hashem, we uncovered this plot when there was still time
for him to escape."

I was weak from the impact of what Rebbe Yitzchak had
just told me.

"But the Rav said that this has to do with the mission we
are on. I don't understand."

Rebbe Yitzchak looked at me. "Avraham, your father will,
with the help of the Almighty, live a long, productive life.
Afterwards, though, who is destined to take his place as the
leader in the area?"

Now, maybe you'll think this is strange, but I didn't know
whom Rebbe Yitzchak could be referring to. I had never even
thought of someone taking over my father's position. Even if I
had, the last person I would imagine in that position was me.
I've already mentioned that I was not the best student, and the

thought of me as the chief rabbi of a section of Eretz Yisrael was simply beyond my imagination. I looked blankly at Rebbe Yitzchak.

He smiled once again. "Avraham, while you might not know the answer to my question, we found out shortly after your father's departure that Abu Rash did. It came to our attention that your father was not the only one he was after. He knew that if your father was not around, you would be next in line, and we think that he therefore decided that you, too, had to go — Heaven forbid."

This revelation did not make me feel any less weak. I'm all for adventure, but this was a little more than I had bargained for. The sun overhead suddenly felt hotter, and my head was beginning to hurt.

"Take a drink from your water bottle, Avraham."

After I did, I felt a little better.

"So that's why I'm here?"

"Yes. You, too, had to be removed from this area quickly, but by the time we realized this, Abu Rash and his men had moved into the area around Yerushalayim. Fleeing secretly as your father did was no longer an option open to us. I understood then that the only available option was to take you out of Eretz Yisrael right under the nose of the fox."

"If I had known what we were doing, I would never have been able to make it. I would have been too afraid."

"Avraham, that is very understandable, and that is why I told you nothing about what we were actually up to."

I realized that my mother had been in on the plan; that's why she'd allowed me to go so easily.

Suddenly, a thought struck me and I was gripped with a

terrible panic. "My mother and sisters — what about them? They are in danger!"

"Rest assured, Avraham, they are in no danger."

"But ..."

"Within minutes of our departure, your mother and sisters were moved to the home of a family that has a lot of girls and aunts living with them; your family will be indistinguishable from them. If anyone comes asking why your home is empty, they will be told that the entire family has left the country. It was decided that for your mother and sisters, this would be safer than traveling around Europe where they could be easily noticed."

My fear began to subside a little. Rebbe Yitzchak had truly planned this out thoroughly.

"So you see, Avraham, we must stay away from Eretz Yisrael until we can somehow get rid of Abu Rash. This is why we have gone on this mission now, despite the fact that I have just recently returned from one."

Not far beneath the surface, I was quite nervous about what Rebbe Yitzchak had just revealed to me. But I knew that keeping my fears there — beneath the surface — for now, instead of letting myself dwell on them, would be the most beneficial thing for me. I needed some time to digest these revelations, and Rebbe Yitzchak realized it.

"You have taken all this amazingly well, my son. I'm truly proud of you. Go now and think it over, and remember that no one, not an Arab sheik nor anyone else, can lift a hand if Hashem does not allow it."

I was burning to ask how it was that we had in fact gotten out from under "the fox's nose." What exactly had happened back there with Abu Rash? I didn't think this was the right time for this question, but I resolved to discuss it later with Rebbe Yitzchak. I thanked him for everything and allowed my camel to fall back slightly, leaving Rebbe Yitzchak to his own thoughts.

Although I was supposed to be thinking over what Rebbe Yitzchak had told me, I didn't have a chance. I noticed that Musa had moved forward and was now riding at my side. "Avraham," he said, "you realize that we have left the Sanjak of Yerushalayim and have entered the Sanjak of Aza."

"Yes, I realized that, Musa."

The Ottoman Empire considers Eretz Yisrael to be part of the province of Syria. At one time, the Ottoman Turks headed the most powerful empire on earth. Nowadays, the empire is far from what it used to be; still, they are the rulers of the land. To make things easier to run, they divided Eretz Yisrael into several districts called Sanjaks. I lived in the Sanjak of Yerushalayim, and Musa was pointing out that we had crossed over into the Sanjak of Aza. I was pretty sure, however, that Musa had more on his mind than this.

After a moment of silence, I saw that I was right.

"I see you were talking with the Rabbi."

"Yes."

"He is a holy man, I think, no?"

"I think so, too."

"How did we get away from Abu Rash? Do you understand?"

"No, I don't."

"He is a holy man, Avraham."

I nodded.

He gave me a smile, and pulled his camel away. "Be well, Avraham."

I was still a little uneasy about him.

I found myself right behind Yaakov and decided to attempt to have a conversation with him. I figured it would be the right thing to do, but I also thought it might distract me from the fact that a powerful sheik was intent on destroying my family. Pulling my camel alongside his, I greeted him.

"How are you, Yaakov?"

He seemed to stiffen. "I'm fine," he answered shortly.

"Quite an adventure we had last night, no?"

He grunted.

I thought to myself that this had to change. I could have a more friendly conversation with Musa than with Yaakov! I was determined to break his shell, or at least to get him to come out of it for a while. I wondered if he knew the real reason for this journey we were on. I decided I would ask Rebbe Yitzchak if I could tell him. Maybe that would help get a conversation started. Maybe.

CHAPTER FOUR

The rest of the trip to Alexandria was basically uneventful, if you consider constant sun, cactus trees and sand uneventful. There was one incident, though, that would not be considered uneventful. I think this incident was the first step in breaking Yaakov's shell, but only the first step.

We had stopped near a village called Sumsum, from where we could see dark caves rising above the desert sand. As Yaakov and I both stood looking at those caves, Musa came over. "Those caves are dangerous," he said.

"What makes them dangerous?" Yaakov asked.

"Sinkholes."

"Sinkholes?" I repeated.

"Yes, Avraham, sinkholes."

"You mean there's water in those caves?" Yaakov asked.

"Not water, quicksand. One can be walking on solid dry earth and suddenly find oneself sinking in quicksand. It's not easy to tell where good solid earth ends and a sinkhole begins, especially in the dim light available in those caves."

"How do you know so much about those sinkholes?" Yaakov wanted to know.

Musa looked at him sharply. "Don't ask me that."

"Why not?"

Yaakov had courage; I'll give him that.

"Listen to me," said Musa. "I've had personal experience with those caves. You have to be careful with them. They can devour people." With that, he turned and left us.

I would not say that I (nor probably Yaakov) really disbelieved what Musa had told us, but I think we felt he was exaggerating somewhat. Besides, we were not going to let his warnings stop us. Curiosity overcame caution, and we started toward the caves. We didn't really go together, because Yaakov barely spoke to me, but we both seemed to have the same idea and went in the same direction.

It was inevitable that we would both enter the same cave, since it was by far the closest one. Although we were not communicating with each other, by some unconscious agreement we both stepped closer as if to ward off any unseen danger. The moment we stepped into the cave, it was as if we were in a different world. While outside the sun shone, inside it was nearly dark. Whereas outside it was hot, inside it was cool. Outside the desert winds blew; inside you could feel the stillness.

We walked on into the cave, trying to look down to see if we were treading on firm earth, but it was very difficult to see in the near darkness. I don't know about Yaakov, but I began to regret my decision to explore the cave. Had I been on my own, I think I would have just turned around and left. But there was no way I was going to look like a coward in front of a fellow who would barely speak to me.

We moved on slowly. As we got deeper into the cave, there was less and less light. I could barely see Yaakov, when I thought I saw him fall. At the same moment, I heard a shriek. My heart started beating quickly. I peered into the darkness, trying to see him. There! Suddenly, I'd caught a glimpse of him. My worst fears were confirmed. He'd fallen into a sink-hole! Then I lost sight of him again, only to spot him again moments later. He was trying to stay afloat in the mud. He tried to scream, but only muffled sounds came out.

I stood absolutely still. I didn't want to fall into that mud.

"Help!" Yaakov managed to scream.

I was near panic. What could I do? Again I heard him calling for help.

I looked around the cave as best as I could. Finally, I spotted what looked like a long wooden pole sticking out of the ground. I wondered if it had once been a tree when a long forgotten opening in the cave had allowed nourishing light to enter. By this time, my eyes had adjusted somewhat to the darkness and I was pretty sure I could see where the quicksand started. Walking very carefully, I made my way around the sinkhole to the tree. I could hear Yaakov splashing and trying to call for help.

"I'm going to help you, Yaakov!" I shouted. "Just see if you can stay afloat for another minute!"

When I got to the pole, I reached into my pocket and pulled out the little knife Moshe had given me. I slashed at the bottom of the pole until it finally came loose. It was long but no wider than a bamboo, so it wasn't that heavy.

Taking the pole, I carefully made my way to the area by the sinkhole closest to where I could still see Yaakov trying his best to cling to life. I held it out, hoping that it would be able to reach Yaakov. I must have been holding my breath, because when I saw that it was long enough to reach Yaakov, I breathed out deeply.

"Yaakov!"

There was no answer. He was concentrating so hard on not getting swallowed up by the mud that he hadn't heard me. I called his name again, and this time he heard me.

"Yaakov, take hold of the tree! Good. Now hold on to your end tightly!"

I pulled on my end as hard as I could. He seemed to move a little closer to me, but not enough. I stopped pulling for a moment to collect my breath, but Yaakov, instead of just hold-ing on, must have been pulling as well, for I felt myself mov-ing. I started pulling again, but it was too late. I'd lost my grip on the solid earth.

I went in with a splash. As I fell in, I heard Yaakov moan. I wondered if this was because he had just lost the only hope he had of being saved, or because he realized that he had inadver-tently pulled me in. I asked Hashem not to let me die there at the bottom of a sinkhole in a dark cave near the village of Sumsum.

It was not easy to move around in that thick soup. Somehow I managed to see that I was near what looked like a large stone. I lunged toward it and somehow got a hold of it. I knew this was my last chance, and I recited a chapter of Tehillim that I knew by heart. I attempted to pull myself up on the ledge with all my might. After what seemed like ages, but must have been only seconds, I found myself on dry earth once again.

I peered into the sinkhole but could not see Yaakov. I didn't hear him either. I was gripped with a great fear. Then I heard him splashing around again. I called out his name, and he managed to answer me. I was startled by how close he sounded. Looking at the sinkhole, I saw that he was not two feet from me.

I thrust myself forward and grabbed him. I got a hold and pulled until he was next to the stone.

"Listen to me, Yaakov," I told him firmly. "You are going to pull yourself up, and at the same time, I am going to pull you, and we are going to finish this crazy business right here and now."

There was no argument from Yaakov, so I said, "Hashem, I hope You see fit to help two silly boys who should have known better." Then I said, "Yaakov, now!"

I had no more strength in me, but I pulled as hard as I could. Then I pulled again, and he was out.

We walked slowly and carefully around the sinkhole until we were on the way out of the cave. When we came out into the bright sun, we looked at each other and realized that we were covered in black from head to toe. I laughed, and then I cried. I think Yaakov did the same. Then we both fell down. An exhausted sleep overtook us instantly.

☾

When we woke up, it was close to nightfall. I felt a lot better than I had when we'd come out of the cave, and I assumed

Yaakov did as well. As we walked back to where our little caravan had camped, Yaakov looked at me and said, "Thank you." Neither of us said anything else.

Rebbe Yitzchak was standing at the edge of the encampment. He looked at us for a moment and then smiled.

"You two very much resemble human beings!" he said. I could imagine what we looked like. Then he grew serious. "I was worried about you. Be more careful next time. Go and wash up and then you will eat something."

As we passed Musa, he said, "You are lucky to be alive. The caves nearly swallowed you, didn't they?"

I didn't think there was much I could say, and apparently, neither did Yaakov. We both nodded without further comment. But Musa had more to say.

"I told you. I have experience with these caves. I was born in this area. I grew up here."

I was surprised to see that Musa seemed to look sad. "I have terrible experience with these caves."

I was waiting for Yaakov to ask Musa about his experience with the caves, but he didn't. No one said anything for a while, and then Musa spoke again. "I lost my brother in there," he said, pointing to the cave we had entered.

"That one?" I asked.

"That very cave. I was in there with him. I could not save him. You have luck. Or you are being watched over."

"I am sorry about your brother, Musa," I said.

"It happened long ago. He, too, was warned not to enter."

There was an uncomfortable silence, and then he turned and walked off.

When Musa had mentioned his brother, it reminded me of

Zerachia. Zerachia was not my natural brother, but he was definitely considered a part of the family. Several years ago, someone discovered that Zerachia, an orphan, was living with an Arab family named Machluf somewhere in Eretz Yisrael and was being raised in a faith other than his own. Somehow — I don't know the details — he had been removed from that home. My father had been approached to take in the boy and guide him through the transition back to living as a Jew. My father and mother had agreed, and Zerachia had become part of our home.

After a while, we heard that the Arab family he'd been living with was trying to locate him, and it was decided that he should study in a yeshivah far from where we lived. By then, Zerachia considered himself part of our family and had excelled in his studies in yeshivah. My father felt that he would be fine on his own. With heavy hearts, we said farewell to him early one morning. We don't know where he went; Rebbe Yitzchak had advised my father that there was less chance of the "other" family locating him if we did not know his whereabouts.

From time to time, he would drop in for a visit. The visits were short and few, but I looked forward to them. Zerachia was older than me and had so completely turned around his life that I really looked up to him. Now, as I watched Musa walking off, I thought of Zerachia. I wondered where he might be at this moment. Did he even know that my father was gone? Probably not.

My thoughts were interrupted by Ahmed, who came over and made some motion that I could not decipher. We went to wash up.

Later, after we'd eaten, I approached Rebbe Yitzchak and

asked if I could speak with him. He was in his tent learning from a *sefer*, as usual. Wherever we were and despite whatever was happening, he learned; it was as if he was able to enter his own private world, free of material distractions.

He motioned for me to sit. "Have you recovered from your adventure, Avraham?" he inquired.

"I think so."

"You certainly look cleaner."

Although in the presence of greatness, one rarely felt ill at ease with Rebbe Yitzchak; he always seemed to know what to say to lighten the atmosphere.

"I can assure Rebbe that I feel cleaner."

"And your friend Yaakov? How is he feeling?"

Was Rebbe Yitzchak calling Yaakov my friend as an ordinary expression, or was he trying to tell me something?

"I think he is suffering no ill effects from our adventure," I said, "although it is hard to imagine how that could be. I thought I'd lost him back there for a moment."

When Rebbe Yitzchak said nothing, I continued, "That is one of the things I wanted to speak to Rebbe about."

"Yaakov?"

"Yes. I want to be his friend. I have tried to be his friend. But he seems to put up a barrier whenever I attempt to talk with him."

"Avraham, that young man has been through a lot in his young life. He is a good boy, as are you. Sometimes, though, when Hashem sends a person difficult challenges, especially when he is so young, it causes that person to build defenses. He doesn't want to be hurt again. Do you understand what I'm saying?"

"I think so. He wants to build a wall to protect himself."

"Yes," Rebbe Yitzchak said, smiling because I'd grasped his point.

"But by doing this, he keeps out not only the bad, but the good as well."

"Avraham, you are correct, but sometimes a person who has suffered makes the decision — at least deep down where he might not even be conscious of it — that it is worth it to keep out the bad, even at the expense of losing the good."

Rebbe Yitzchak's words made me even more determined to get through to "my friend" Yaakov.

"Does Yaakov know the reason for this journey?"

"Do you mean about you and your father and Abu Rash?"

"Yes."

"I don't think he does."

"Can I tell him? Perhaps it will help me get through to him."

"I don't see why not. He is a trustworthy young man. I think you will find you have much in common with him."

When I said nothing, Rebbe Yitzchak continued, "But Avraham, did you come here to speak only of your friend? What about you?"

"There are things on my mind, but I don't know if this is the right time ..."

"What better time could there be? You are here. I am here. It is the perfect time." He smiled.

"I am ashamed of the fact that I am afraid."

"Afraid?"

"Yes. I am a coward. I am afraid of danger."

Rebbe Yitzchak laughed. "Forgive me, Avraham, but who is not?"

I didn't know what to answer.

"Avraham, fear is given to a person in the same way as the sensation of pain is given to a person. If one wouldn't feel pain when touching fire, one would not immediately remove one's finger from the fire, and one would get terribly burned. Fear is the same; it pushes us to stay away from danger. Hashem gave us both instincts to protect ourselves. Only when it controls us and prevents us from doing what is right is fear a bad thing."

"I think perhaps in my case it stops me from doing what is right."

"Give me an example, Avraham."

"Well, in the cave, when Yaakov fell in, I panicked," I said, as the scene replayed itself in my mind. "I didn't want to suffer the same fate."

Rebbe Yitzchak's face turned almost angry. "Avraham, how did Yaakov get out?"

I was silent.

"You risked your life to save him! Avraham, don't let the *yetzer hara* befuddle you. You risked your life to save another Jew, and you are afraid that you are a coward?"

I had rarely heard Rebbe Yitzchak speak so forcefully. Then his tone softened. "Avraham, one can work on dealing with fear, but if you ever meet someone who claims to naturally have no fear, what do you know about him?" He answered his own question. "Avraham, you know that he is either a liar, or someone who has lost his senses."

There was silence for a moment, and then Rebbe Yitzchak asked, "Do you hear me, Avraham?"

"Yes," I said, and I really did.

"So, Avraham, what else should we speak about?"

"I have other types of fears."

"Tell me."

"I fear that I can never measure up to my father. He is a great *talmid chacham*, and he expects me to be one as well. I am not a very good student. I'm afraid I will disappoint him."

"Avraham, you have what it takes to be great. That's all I can say. Put in the effort, ask Hashem for assistance, and you will grow to make your father proud. I have seen much weaker students than you become great with some effort. You too, Avraham, will succeed."

Although I still had my doubts about my ever being able to make my father proud of my accomplishments in learning, I felt much lighter after Rebbe Yitzchak's words. I did not plan to burden him with more questions, but he asked, "*Nu*, what else shall we discuss?"

"Will I ever see my father again?"

"With the help of Hashem you will."

"How will this all end? How can we ever rid ourselves of Abu Rash? How will we ever be able to return to Eretz Yisrael?"

"Avraham, those are all good questions. I remind you, though, that Abu Rash cannot lift a finger if the Almighty does not allow it."

I hesitated for a moment, wondering if I should voice a feeling I had.

"What is it, Avraham?"

"Rebbe said that the reason Abu Rash is after my father and me is in order to have unquestioned control over the area outside Yerushalayim."

"Yes, Avraham, this is what we have been told."

"I don't know ... it's just that I can't help feeling that there's more to it than that. I mean, I'm sure that's part of it, but somehow, deep inside me, I wonder if there's something else."

"Like what, Avraham?"

"I don't know. It's just a feeling. It scares me, because if he just wants us out of the way, then if we stay out of his way long enough he might not pursue us, but if he has something else against us then ..."

"Listen, Avraham, you are a smart young man and I am not going to pretend that I can fully explain Abu Rash's motivations. I am also not going to try to tell you that I have not wondered the same thing as you have. Abu Rash is clearly bent on finding both you and your father, and while his desire for power explains this somewhat, I must admit that I, too, am not convinced that we know the full story."

What Rebbe Yitzchak said should have made me more nervous, but the truth is, it had the opposite effect on me. I think that realizing that Rebbe Yitzchak was validating my fears and not trying to sugarcoat the situation actually made me feel calmer.

"But Avraham, that does not change what we've said until now. Whatever Abu Rash's motives are, he has power only as long as Hashem allows him to have power."

"Can I ask one more thing, or is it —"

"Ask!"

"How were we able to escape from Abu Rash? I thought I heard the Rav saying something to himself ...."

"We don't talk about these things. You should know that

while the hidden Torah is a great *chachmah*, we rarely use it practically."

"But under certain circumstances —"

"What is important is that Hashem is One, and there is no other. We spoke before about removing fear. Well, when a person realizes that Hashem is One, and that nobody can hurt him if He doesn't allow it, how can he fear? It is not just miracles I am speaking of, Avraham. When one thinks of Hashem, he is calm. Hashem can send miracles in hidden ways."

Rebbe Yitzchak paused, looked at his *sefer* and said, "Avraham, I must learn more now. If I do not, I will remain ignorant."

I waited for his smile, but there was none. He was completely serious.

I stood up and said, "Good night, and thank you for the *chizuk*."

"Good night, Avraham, sleep well."

I left the tent feeling as if I'd had an audience with the *Urim v'Tumim*.

CHAPTER FIVE

After about two months of traveling, we arrived in the city of Alexandria. Our first moments there were not very promising. As we entered the city, we passed a large procession of Turkish soldiers who were apparently accompanying a high level Turkish Pasha (government official). The commotion they made did not at all agree with our pack mules, and they went into a frenzy. The camels began to get a bit wild as well, and for a moment I thought we'd be thrown off. It took us several minutes to calm them all down.

I noted with interest that the Ottomans still had a military presence in Egypt. Although officially Egypt was under Turkish rule, the country had been moving toward independence from Turkey for a while. This was part of the general weakening of the empire. If you're wondering why such a mighty empire was slowly losing its strength, I think a lot of it has to do with the fact that the local Ottoman officials had become awfully corrupt. Back in Eretz Yisrael, we had to bribe officials to get just about anything done. And this was in addition to the official taxes, like the money we paid to be exempt from serving in the army.

Once things had settled down, we were able to make our way to the home of a distinguished Jew by the name of Reb Chaim Provencal, who welcomed us with open arms. Although we were a little tired, he insisted on taking us to a *beis kenesses* a short distance from the city. It was known as the *beis kenesses* of Eliyahu, for they have a tradition that Eliyahu Hanavi once appeared there. It was a very imposing building with twenty-six marble pillars.

On the way back, Reb Chaim said, "Rebbe Yitzchak, disturbing news has just reached me from Eretz Yisrael."

"Oh?" said Rebbe Yitzchak, turning to him.

"Apparently, there was a young Jewish boy from Yerushalayim who was not getting along very well with his family. He was not studying properly and was acting up in various ways. It seems that several of the Greek Orthodox priests who live in the city befriended him. Now it appears that the boy has disappeared and it is strongly suspected that the priests have taken him away."

"We don't usually have trouble from them," Rebbe Yitzchak said sadly, "but one never knows from where the test will come."

I knew what Rebbe Yitzchak meant. Lately, many Protestant missionaries had come to Yerushalayim from

Britain and the United States, and they sometimes proved troublesome. Generally, though, the Greek Orthodox priests in their long black robes and caps and beards kept to themselves. An incident like this was unusual.

"Let us pray that the boy is found," said Rebbe Yitzchak, "and that he be able to work out whatever is bothering him."

We rode on in silence.

By the time we returned to Alexandria, the day was already drawing to a close. I was quite tired, and after Maariv and some supper I was shown to my room. It had been a while since I'd slept under a solid roof. Of course, we'd slept in some of the villages along the way, but not in a comfortable house like this. To tell you the truth, I'm not sure I'd ever slept in a house like this. This was not to be the largest home we would stay in during our journey, but at the time it seemed big to me.

☾

The next morning as Rebbe Yitzchak sat learning in the Provencal salon, he suggested that Yaakov and I learn as well. We did so, but not together. Afterwards, I wanted to explore the city. I tried to get Yaakov to come with me, but he declined, so I set out on my own.

I mentioned my Uncle Gavriel earlier, and now I'll tell you a little about him. Uncle Gavriel made a living by growing long-fibered cotton in various places in Eretz Yisrael. This strain of cotton used to be a productive crop in Eretz Yisrael, but since it started being grown in Egypt decades ago it pretty much lost its value in our land. Now, however, with civil war raging in America and many battles taking place on the great American cotton fields, long-fibered cotton grown in Eretz Yisrael once again became a valuable item.

How, you might ask, did my uncle know how to grow long-fibered cotton? It's true he owns a farm, but how did he suddenly know how to grow a crop that hasn't been grown in the area for decades? The answer is, my uncle knows everything, or at least that's the way it seems to me. Whenever I talk to him, he is literally overflowing with information on every imaginable subject. He often tells me about various places around the globe. One place he told me about was the city of Alexandria.

Uncle Gavriel told me that Alexandria is built on a long isthmus (strip of land) between Lake Maryut and the Mediterranean Sea. A peninsula shaped like a hammer sticks out of the isthmus forming two large harbors, east and west. These grand harbors have made the city one of the Mediterranean's major ports for ages. I wanted to see the harbors and the rest of the city I had heard so much about.

The best way to describe the city is to say that it was alive. There was movement everywhere. Merchants selling their wares called out for customers, as did people selling various types of food. It reminded me of the market in my town, only it was bigger. This led me to think about my town, which made me a little sad. I tried to distract myself by looking around at all the activity.

That's when we saw each other.

Across the street from me stood a man I immediately recognized as a member of Abu Rash's gang. We had looked into each other's eyes that evening when we'd met Abu Rash face to face, and now we were doing so again. His eyes widened as he looked at me, and he started across the street toward me. Something told me that I did not want to stay and see what he had to say. Without much thought, I ran.

Nearly bumping into several people, I continued running, trying to find somewhere I could hide. The entranceway of every building I passed seemed to be blocked by people, and I didn't want to push my way in, fearing that perhaps I would be stopped. As I ran, I quickly glanced back and saw that he was right behind me! I figured that he would catch up to me in several seconds.

Then I saw the open doorway.

A large wooden door stood wide open with no one blocking the entrance, and I entered the building. I realized immediately that I was in a mosque. Arab men kneeled on mats in prayer. I glanced at the doorway and saw that my pursuer had not followed me in. I remembered what I learned in the name of the Rambam, that one could enter a mosque if necessary. Again I glanced at the doorway; it seemed he was not going to follow me in. I was pretty sure, though, that he would be waiting for me when I came out.

I noticed a little hallway at the side of the room, and I headed there to get out of view of the mosque's occupants. It was much darker there. My heart was beating so fast that I was afraid it would burst. How was I going to get out of there without Abu Rash's man seeing me? I knew that as long as I stayed inside, he would still be waiting for me. Besides, how long could I stay unnoticed in this little dark hallway?

I'm not sure how long I stood there with my heart beating away. Then I remembered my discussion with Rebbe Yitzchak, and I took a deep breath. *It is not just miracles I am speaking of, Avraham,* he had said. *When one thinks of Hashem, he is calm. Hashem can send miracles in hidden ways.* My heart began to slow, and I grew calmer. I was still very much aware of the fact that there was a fellow outside waiting for me, who probably didn't mean me very well, but I had calmed down a little.

There was barely any light in the hallway. I started feeling my way around to see if I could possibly find some room to hide in. I felt the cool stone give way to wood, and realized I was in front of a door. Gently, I opened it and went through the doorway. I found myself in a large room with not much more light than the hallway. A noise at my right startled me and something hit my arm. I jumped. I realized that I had just been swatted by the tail of an animal. Straining to look around, I figured out that I was in a type of stable.

Moving carefully past a wagon full of hay and a sleepy looking mule, I walked to the other end of the stable. There was a door. I tried it and it opened slightly, letting in sunlight. I immediately shut it. Now I figured that since this barn door was in the back of the mosque, it probably opened onto a different street. I told myself that since I'd be leaving from a different exit, a different building and a different street, I would be able to escape. I could just slip out that door and run back to the Provencal home.

I was about to open the door again and leave, when a frightening thought came to me. What if Abu Rash's man knew more than I thought he did? What if he knew there was another way out of the mosque? What if he was waiting right outside?

I looked around the stable in the dim light. In a far corner I found what I was looking for. There, slung over a barrel, was a hooded robe frequently worn by mule drivers. I put it on, covering my face as much as possible. Then I went over to the hay wagon and tried to harness the mule to it. I silently thanked Hashem for the summer I had spent on my Uncle Gavriel's farm in the north.

With my heart in my mouth, I led the mule and the wagon it was pulling toward the large stable door. I said a *tefillah* and opened the door. Without looking to see who might be standing there, I closed the stable door. As I climbed up on the wagon, I saw him standing a few yards away from me. I shuddered. He was glancing this way and that. I understood that he had in fact known about this exit, and was apparently standing at a spot from where he could watch both exits.

It's not easy praying desperately while you're trying to look as if you were a wagon driver doing his job without a care in the world. If he recognized me, I was finished. Even if he didn't, if someone familiar with the stable came along, I was also finished. As I started urging the mule to go, I saw him looking at me. I hoped that my face was covered enough. I wondered if I could get the mule to go fast enough to outrun him if he started chasing me. I was so frightened that I was shaking; I hoped he didn't notice.

The mule began to move. My back was now to the man. As the wagon moved along the street, I expected to hear him yelling for me to stop. He did. My heart jumped. I wondered if I should try to run, but then he was right there beside the wagon.

"Listen," he said, "did you see a young Jew in there?"

I laughed. "In there? Never."

He grunted and went back to his watching post. I guess I really looked like an Arab wagon driver.

I thought of Rebbe Yitzchak. *Hashem can send miracles in hidden ways.*

CHAPTER SIX

When I returned to the Provencal home, I was told that Rebbe Yitzchak was talking to our host in his study. I knocked and was told to enter. Although I had other things on my mind, I noticed that there was an extensive collection of *sefarim* in the room. When Rebbe Yitzchak saw that I was hesitant to talk in front of Reb Chaim, he said, "Our host can hear whatever you have to say, Avraham."

He then looked at me closely. "Are you all right, Avraham?"

"I am, *baruch Hashem*, fine now, but I wasn't so sure I would be fine a little while back."

"What happened, young man?" Reb Chaim asked.

"I ran into a man I recognized from Abu Rash's gang."

"And he recognized you as well?" Rebbe Yitzchak inquired.

"Yes."

For the next several minutes, I related every detail of my adventure down to the fact that there was a wagon and mule now standing in front of the Provencal home. Reb Chaim immediately called for one of his aides. "I'm sure you are aware of the wagon in front," he said.

"Yes, sir, I am."

"Please have it returned to the Amdan stable."

"Yes, sir, right away. How shall I explain how it came to be here?"

"Tell them I will explain everything shortly. My first concern is to return the wagon and mule."

The man left the study.

"Reb Chaim," said Rebbe Yitzchak, "the question is this. I must stay here in Alexandria for a short time. In your opinion, is it safe for us to remain here?"

Reb Chaim thought for a moment and said, "I will dispense with false modesty, since there is no time for it. I am quite sure that my influence in this city is such that if you stay at my home, you are safe. I do not think that Abu Rash's man will dare to bother you while you are under my protection. If he would, the local authorities would come down hard on him."

"Very well, we will stay for now."

This decision made me a bit nervous, but of course I didn't say so.

After I rested a bit, I went out to the yard behind the Provencal home. I found Yaakov sitting under a tree, and I sat down nearby. I was not expecting any conversation, but I was in for a bit of a surprise.

"I heard that you had a close call. I was happy to hear that you were all right."

I could barely believe my ears. "Thanks," I said. "It was one of Abu Rash's men. I recognized him and apparently he recognized me."

"He is no good, no good at all."

"Who are you talking about, Yaakov?"

"Who? Abu Rash, that's who. He and his men are ruthless."

"Yes, that's what I've heard."

"It's true, believe me."

I could tell that there was more he wanted to say, but could not decide if he should. Suddenly, we were interrupted by a commotion in the house. We got up to see what was happening.

Inside we found Rebbe Yitzchak at the table; he had apparently just looked up from his *sefer*. In front of him stood our host. To the side stood Musa. On either side of him stood one of the Provencals' housemen. They seemed to each have a hold of one of Musa's arms.

"Rebbe Yitzchak," Reb Chaim was saying, "I ask your forgiveness for the interruption, but I felt that this was important."

Rebbe Yitzchak looked at Musa. "Why are they restraining him?"

"That is exactly why I have come, Rebbe Yitzchak. Several minutes ago, one of my men came to tell me that he had noticed this Musa looking around in one of my wife's jewelry cases. I quickly came to investigate, but he had already left the room. We quietly followed him, and were shocked to find him in your room, Rebbe Yitzchak. He was going through your valise!

"We watched in silence as he pulled out an envelope, looked inside, and then pocketed it. He then closed the valise and was about to leave the room, when we confronted him. My men searched him and found this."

Reb Chaim pulled a silver pin from his pocket.

"They continued searching him and found this."

He now pulled out an envelope, from which I could see money sticking out. I don't know why, but somehow the situation struck me as funny. Reb Chaim was standing there with a lady's pin in one hand and an envelope of money in the other. Musa was standing between two men, looking grim. Rebbe Yitzchak sat surveying the whole situation. From our corner Yaakov and I watched to see what would happen.

I tried with all my might to suppress the laugh that was straining to get out of me. All of my efforts paid off. Instead of a loud belly laugh, I let out what might have been interpreted as a strong sigh of despair. Rebbe Yitzchak gave me a look that was enough to silence any upcoming laughter.

My strange sense of humor aside, though, there was a rather uncomfortable atmosphere in the room. Everyone seemed tense, except for me, who for some reason still felt like laughing.

"I must tell you," said Rebbe Yitzchak, his face serious, "that I have suspected something like this for a while. Things have been disappearing for some time now."

There was silence in the room. Now even I felt the tension.

Rebbe Yitzchak looked at Musa. "You probably are not

able to repay what you have stolen in the past."

"No, sir, I do not have money to repay."

Reb Chaim spoke up. "I presume that you will have him leave your employ immediately."

Rebbe Yitzchak sighed. "I suppose so."

Reb Chaim looked at the two men who stood at either side of Musa. "Men," he said, and they started moving Musa out the door.

Rebbe Yitzchak looked at Musa. "I want you to know that, aside from stealing, you have done service to me, Musa, and I appreciate it."

Musa nodded.

I really had mixed feelings at this point. I'd been suspicious of Musa from the start, and his dismissal shouldn't have bothered me. On the other hand, he seemed to have a certain decency. Although I knew that Rebbe Yitzchak really had little choice but to let him go, I was a little sad at the turn of events.

Yaakov and I followed the three men out of the room. We watched as Musa was unceremoniously escorted out of the house and the door slammed behind him. We opened the door a crack and watched Musa slowly walk away.

"Be well, Musa," I called.

He turned. "You two should know something. I told you about my brother, do you remember?"

"Yes, he died in the cave," Yaakov said.

"He was the older brother; I was still young at the time. We had no father. When he died, I had to support my mother and sisters. Work was not easy to come by for a young boy like me. I began to steal."

There was silence, until he continued, "You get used to

stealing; it becomes second nature. It is best not to start."

He waved, and then continued down the road.

So that's how our caravan got a little smaller.

We were not planning to leave Alexandria right away; Rebbe Yitzchak seemed to be waiting for something. I decided to stay as close as possible to Reb Chaim's home. I had no interest in meeting my friend from Abu Rash's gang again. I suggested to Yaakov that he do the same. I got no argument from him.

Having had a rather active day, I went to sleep early. Before I fell asleep, I thought of my mother and sisters. As I slept, I dreamed of my father. I asked him what he would do if I did not end up becoming a great *talmid chacham*. I also asked him when I would be able to see him in real life. He didn't answer either of my questions, for he was too far away.

CHAPTER SEVEN

The next day, our suspicions about Abu Rash were confirmed.

Yaakov was not feeling very well and was resting. Rebbe Yitzchak and I were sitting alone in the Provencal dining room having a bite to eat, when a houseman entered and gave Rebbe Yitzchak a note. "I was given this to give the Rabbi," he said.

"Who gave it to you?" asked Rebbe Yitzchak.

"Another rabbi," said the houseman, "but he was dressed in European clothes."

"A broad hat and a black coat?"

"Yes, Rabbi."

Rebbe Yitzchak looked at me. "Sounds like an Ashkenazi *rav*," he commented.

As he read the note, he seemed to be taken aback. Looking up, he said, "This was written by a *talmid chacham* who is knowledgeable in both the revealed and the hidden Torah. He does not give his name, but says that he has something to tell us. He wants us to stay here for the next hour so that we will be in when he comes."

It turned out that we did not have to wait an hour, for shortly the houseman asked Rebbe Yitzchak if he would see the guest.

"Yes," said Rebbe Yitzchak, "show him in."

He returned a moment later with a tall man dressed in the garb of the Ashkenazi *perushim* of Yerushalayim. The man had a long black beard and a faraway look in his eyes.

"*Shalom aleichem*," Rebbe Yitzchak greeted him.

"*Aleichem shalom*," answered the man, as he shook Rebbe Yitzchak's outstretched hand.

"You are from Eretz Yisrael?" Rebbe Yitzchak asked as he motioned for the man to sit down at the table with us.

"I am indeed, as I believe are the Rav and this young man."

It wasn't clear if he was asking or telling.

"What is your name?"

"My name is Yekusiel."

I thought it strange that he gave no last name, but Rebbe Yitzchak didn't seem to notice.

"Where did you study?"

"Why does the Rav ask?"

"From your note, it is clear that you studied with someone great."

"I have studied with many great men, *baruch Hashem*."

"You have studied the secrets of the Torah."

Rebbe Yitzchak said this as a statement rather than a question.

"With Reb Yosef of Tzefas."

I didn't recognize the name, but Rebbe Yitzchak smiled. "I see. You live in Tzefas?"

"Yes, I do."

"Welcome, then, Rebbe Yekusiel of Tzefas."

Rebbe Yekusiel nodded in acknowledgement of the greeting.

"To what do we owe the honor of this visit, Rebbe Yekusiel?"

Rebbe Yekusiel looked at me. "You are Rebbe Daniel's son, are you not?"

"Yes," I said, wondering how he knew.

"I know Rebbe Daniel," he said, turning back to Rebbe Yitzchak, "or at least I knew him many years ago when we both studied with Rebbe Suleiman, may his memory be blessed. It has been a long time since we've spoken. Rebbe Daniel's son looks as he himself looked years ago."

"Really?" I asked. "So much so that you were actually able to recognize me?"

Our guest turned back to me and smiled. "Well, I did recognize you, did I not?"

I nodded.

Looking again at Rebbe Yitzchak, he said, "As I've said, I live in Tzefas in the north of Eretz Yisrael. I know that the reasons for your mission are not supposed to be public knowledge, but I am aware of them."

"I will not ask how you know," said Rebbe Yitzchak, "but

do tell us how that explains your visit today."

The man hesitated and then said, "Certainly, the Rav is aware that Abu Rash's base of operations is in the north."

"Yes," said Rebbe Yitzchak, "we are aware of that."

"One day, I overheard two men talking. I happen to know that they were members of Abu Rash's group. They were talking about Rebbe Daniel."

My heart jumped. "What were they saying?" I asked anxiously.

"One of them said, 'This is really personal with the boss. He really has it against this rabbi.' The other said, 'That's true. I actually heard him say that he would never forgive or forget.'"

I felt weak. Our suspicions were true; Abu Rash had some sort of vendetta against my father.

"When I heard you were here," Rebbe Yekusiel continued, "I thought that it would be best to let you know about this. It is not simply that Abu Rash wants Rebbe Daniel out of Eretz Yisrael; it is something more than that. I thought you should know that, as it might help you in formulating how to deal with the situation."

"Yes, you did the right thing," Rebbe Yitzchak agreed. "The more we know, the better prepared we are to deal with the situation. We had already suspected as much, but you have now confirmed our suspicions. Tell me, though, Rebbe Yekusiel, do you have any idea what kind of grudge this man has against Rebbe Daniel?"

"No, unfortunately, I do not. After that brief exchange, the men moved on and I lost them. I tried asking around, but I was not able to obtain any more information."

There was silence in the room for a moment.

"And why are you here in Alexandria?" Rebbe Yitzchak finally asked.

"As Rebbe Yitzchak knows better than most, everyone has their own mission," our guest said simply.

I wondered if Rebbe Yitzchak would press him for a more specific answer, but he didn't.

I was feeling pretty down and my face must have showed it, because Rebbe Yitzchak said, "Avraham, this changes nothing, nothing at all. Hashem can deal with the likes of Abu Rash whatever his reasons for chasing your father are."

Turning to Rebbe Yekusiel he asked, "Are you certain that that's all you overheard? Any piece of information we have may prove useful."

Rebbe Yekusiel seemed to consider something for a moment. "There was one more thing," he said thoughtfully.

"Well," said Rebbe Yitzchak, with what might possibly have been a trace of annoyance in his voice, "tell us what it was."

"They said something as they were leaving, but I did not hear it fully. That is why I hesitate to say it —"

"Rebbe Yekusiel, I would ask you to stop holding us in suspense and tell us already," Rebbe Yitzchak said with what might have either been a smile or a frown. I couldn't tell which one it was.

"I think that one of the men said, 'This rabbi is certainly a high priority project for the boss.'" Rebbe Yekusiel looked at me before he continued. "Then the other one said, 'Yes, and I hear that his son is an even higher priority than he is.'"

"This keeps getting worse and worse," I said in despair.

"Listen, Avraham, we already knew that they were interested in you as well," Rebbe Yitzchak said.

"Yes, but why would I be more important to them than my father?"

"That I do not know, Avraham," said Rebbe Yitzchak. He turned back to our guest. "You heard nothing else, Rebbe Yekusiel?"

"Nothing at all."

"I see," Rebbe Yitzchak said. "Then can I perhaps ask the houseman to bring you something to eat?"

"No, although I appreciate the offer," Rebbe Yekusiel answered, getting to his feet. "I must be going now. I wish you *hatzlachah* in outwitting this Abu Rash."

"And may you have *hatzlachah* in your mission, whatever it may be," Rebbe Yitzchak said, smiling. "We truly appreciate the information you have given us, Rebbe Yekusiel."

Rebbe Yekusiel gave a little wave and, as quickly as he had come, he was gone. After he left, Rebbe Yitzchak said, "There are still things about this situation that we do not understand, but you know what I do understand, Avraham?"

I smiled. "There is only One?"

"Exactly."

"Could I ask how Rebbe knew by reading his note that he was a *talmid chacham*?"

"Avraham, there is much one can tell about a person by reading what he has written."

"It's interesting that he sent a note before he came, isn't it?" I remarked. "Perhaps he wanted Rebbe to see his writing before meeting him so that Rebbe would trust him and be more likely to accept what he was saying."

"Perhaps," said Rebbe Yitzchak, "perhaps."

CHAPTER EIGHT

We spent another two days in Alexandria, during which Rebbe Yitzchak went to the local telegraph office several times. I wondered whom he was telegraphing, but of course, I didn't ask. Yaakov and I talked a little more, but he still wasn't ready to really let down his guard.

We were both sitting in the yard behind Reb Chaim's home when I told him about my father's flight from Eretz Yisrael and the reason for our journey. I started with an account of Rebbe Yekusiel's visit and the information he had given us. When I described Rebbe Yekusiel, I saw a gleam of recognition in his eyes.

"Yes, I saw him on his way out the other day," he said. "I was just getting up from a nap and I saw an Ashkenazi *rav* leaving the house."

"That was him."

When I'd finished summarizing what we knew, I noticed a dark shadow come over Yaakov's face.

"What is it, Yaakov?"

"You can't imagine how I hate him."

"Abu Rash, I presume?"

"That's right."

I thought that he was about to tell me his story, but he said nothing else. I realized that this conversation was very much like another I had had with Yaakov recently. Then, too, he had expressed rage at Abu Rash but had stopped short of explaining himself. I was wondering what I should say, when Ahmed came over and motioned for us to follow him.

He led us into the house and to Rebbe Yitzchak's room. There we found Rebbe Yitzchak packing. When he heard us, he looked up and smiled. "You are just the people I wanted to see."

"What is it, Rebbe?" I asked.

"Tomorrow morning we sail for Livorno in Italy."

"What will we do with our camels and mules?" Yaakov asked.

"That is taken care of. We need only to pack our belongings and be ready in the morning for Reb Chaim's driver to take us to the port."

"Does Rebbe need any help packing?"

He smiled. "Avraham, help comes from the One Above."

We left his room excited that we were soon to begin the next part of our journey.

Immediately after *tefillah* and a quick bite, we boarded the wagon with our things. There were two mules attached to the wagon and we were ready to go, except that there was no driver in sight. Reb Chaim came out and Rebbe Yitzchak began to get up. Reb Chaim waved him to remain seated.

"Don't bother to get up, Rebbe Yitzchak," he said.

"I wanted to express our appreciation for all —"

"You will have an opportunity to say whatever you would like to say, as we travel."

"You are coming, too?" Rebbe Yitzchak asked.

"Yes," said Reb Chaim, climbing up into the driver's seat.

"I don't understand," Rebbe Yitzchak said. "Where will the driver sit?"

Reb Chaim smiled. "He will sit where he is now sitting."

"You don't mean —"

"Yes, Rebbe Yitzchak, that's exactly what I mean. If anyone thinks that I would let a mere driver take such a distinguished guest to the port, he is quite mistaken."

"I will not allow it," Rebbe Yitzchak declared. "It is not befitting your honor."

"On the contrary," Reb Chaim said, "it is my honor to drive you. Besides, I did not arrange for a driver. How else will you get there?" He gave a little laugh and started the mules forward.

"You outsmarted me, Reb Chaim. Had I known of your plan, I would never have agreed," Rebbe Yitzchak said, resigned to the situation.

It was not a very long drive to the port, and soon we were there. I marveled at the harbor that was every bit as magnificent as my uncle had described. As Reb Chaim helped us bring our things to the cargo masters, he thanked Rebbe Yitzchak for the opportunity to have been his host.

"It is I who have to thank you for your unparalleled hospitality. Please convey to your *eishes chayil* our appreciation for all of her efforts. May you only have good tidings."

"Amen," Reb Chaim said. "And please promise me that if you come this way again, you will stay with us."

Rebbe Yitzchak agreed, and then we were on our way up the ramp to the ship. Neither Yaakov nor I had ever been at sea, and we could barely contain our excitement. As we entered the ship, one of the seamen, a man with large, intense eyes, seemed to stand out from the rest. I would later learn that he was the captain of the ship. Right away I knew he would be a cause of trouble.

We didn't have to wait long for some excitement on board. During our second night at sea, a powerful storm came upon us. For hours the wind howled and the rain came down in torrents. Thunder crackled all around us, and the black night was lit up with brilliant flashes of lightning. The ship tossed one way and then another, and I was desperately scared for my life.

I was sitting with Yaakov in the cabin we shared, hoping for the storm to pass, when there was a knock on the door. I opened it and was surprised to see Rebbe Yitzchak standing there.

"Is Rebbe all right?" I asked.

"*Baruch Hashem*, I am fine. I've come to check on you two. I have been at sea several times before, and this is not my first storm. They can be quite unsettling, and I wanted to see how you were."

"When will it pass already?" Yaakov asked nervously.

"Soon enough. We are riding against the storm and not

with it, so we should be behind the storm in a little while."

"Is there danger to the ship?" I asked.

"As I've said, I have been through storms like this before, and with Hashem's help, I am still here to tell you about it."

Just then, the ship leaned sharply to one side, and Rebbe Yitzchak nearly stumbled. Yaakov and I rushed to his aid, but he had already caught himself. "I didn't say that it wasn't a rough ride," he said, smiling, "only that it will soon be over."

He turned to go. "Remember, my sons, Hashem is One, there is no other."

"We will help Rebbe back to his cabin," I said.

"No," he said firmly. "It will be safer for you to stay where you are."

We watched him wave to us and then leave.

"If it's safer for us to stay in one place, then it's also safer for Rebbe Yitzchak to stay in one place," Yaakov commented.

"Yet he went out of his way to visit us, because he knew we'd be frightened," I said, finishing Yaakov's thought.

Just then we heard another knock on the door. "Is it Rebbe Yitzchak again?" I asked Yaakov in a whisper. He shrugged to indicate that he didn't know.

I opened the door. Ahmed stood in the doorway, looking frightened. Through a whole series of hand motions he somehow explained to us that he had gone out to see if the storm was getting any lighter, and had found himself too scared to find his way back to his cabin. Apparently, our cabin was on the way, so he had knocked to ask for our assistance.

Yaakov and I looked at each other. Neither of us felt like

walking around the ship in the storm, but how could we refuse the terrified man?

"I'll go," I offered.

"I'll come, too," Yaakov said.

Ahmed bowed his head as if to thank us, and the three of us started down the corridor. I realized how difficult it must have been for Rebbe Yitzchak to come visit us. While sitting in a cabin during a storm was frightening, walking through the ship in a storm was truly terrifying. The ship lurched from side to side, and we had to steady ourselves by holding on firmly to the walls.

Finally, we reached Ahmed's cabin. Before we left him there, he made a deep bow of appreciation. I don't know about Yaakov, but it made me feel uncomfortable. I mean, what was so great about what we'd just done? Who wouldn't have done the same?

"All right," Yaakov said as we headed toward our cabin. "Now we have to make it back."

"Well," I said, "if we made it here, we can make it back."

It wasn't so easy, though. They say that there is calm before the storm. Well, it seems that sometimes, the opposite is also true; before the storm calms down, it really gets itself all worked up. There were times when the ship leaned so far down that it seemed that it was lying on its side. The way back from Ahmed's cabin definitely seemed harder than the way to his cabin.

At one point, when the ship made an especially sharp turn to the side, Yaakov fell. I tried to grab him, and also ended up falling. Neither of us was hurt, but it was far from a pleasant experience. When we were both back on our feet, we were startled to find ourselves face to face with one of the ship's mates.

"What are you doing here?" he demanded.

"Going back to our cabin," I said.

"Well, get back to the cabin and stay there if you know what's good for you!"

Neither of us argued. We continued on our way, and with help from Above we somehow made it back to our cabin. Exhausted, we sat down on our bunks. The storm began to grow less angry within the hour, and we were soon asleep.

CHAPTER NINE

It was during our second week at sea that Rebbe Yitzchak noticed many of our food provisions had become infested with tiny worms. We attempted to separate whatever had not been infested to save it from the worms. This was no easy task. In Rebbe Yitzchak's cabin, the creatures seemed to be everywhere. Our cabin was not much better. Rebbe Yitzchak did not want to use Ahmed's cabin, although from what we could decipher from Ahmed's hand motions, his cabin was not too clean either.

Rebbe Yitzchak managed to buy rice from another traveler to help carry us through the rest of the trip. The price he paid was well above what it should have been, but there was little choice. The infestation in Rebbe Yitzchak's cabin got so bad that he finally asked that he be assigned another room.

We were surprised when permission was granted, and we got word that he could move to an unoccupied cabin in a different part of the ship.

On a cold windy night, we helped Rebbe Yitzchak move his things to the new cabin. It was about the same size as the other cabin, but it was farther away from the one where Yaakov and I were staying. It did seem to be less wormy, though. Rebbe Yitzchak thanked us for our help and wished us a good night. It was late and we soon went to sleep.

Early the next morning, Ahmed was at our door. He seemed excited and insisted that we come with him. He led us to Rebbe Yitzchak's old cabin. A ship's mate stood in the doorway, looking in. When he heard us coming, he said, "Your rabbi sure has luck." When we asked what he meant, he motioned for us to look inside the cabin.

The sight that greeted us was chilling. A large wooden chest that had stood near the bunk had somehow collapsed. It now lay in pieces all over the bunk.

"If someone would have been sleeping there when it fell ..."

The ship's mate did not finish his thought; he didn't have to.

We rushed to Rebbe Yitzchak's new cabin to tell him what had happened. When he heard what we had to say, he smiled. "It is said that the Almighty has many messengers. Apparently, the worms carried out their mission well. Let us hope that we carry out our missions as well as they did."

The rest of our trip on the Mediterranean Sea was not very exciting — except that something happened to Yaakov and the two of us became real friends. Being on a ship for so long can get a little boring, and we used to take walks around the ship to see if we could find anything interesting.

Once, we saw two ship's mates who seemed to have some
free time on their hands. They were playing some sort of
game, which we had never seen in Eretz Yisrael. One mate
would roll a heavy looking metal ball across the deck to the
other, and the other mate would roll it back to him. If each
was able to catch the metal ball and send it back, the game
continued. But if one let it get by him, he lost the game and
the other was the winner.

"It looks interesting," I said.

"If you have nothing else to do, yes," Yaakov added.

"Well, it's true that Rebbe Yitzchak makes sure we learn
every day, but we do have some free time."

"I'm not arguing. With nothing much else to do on board,
it would definitely be something to try."

"You think we could ask them if we could borrow the ball
sometime?"

"We could try. They seem to be nice enough fellows."

We watched the game until one of the men was out.

"Nice game," Yaakov said to them.

The men turned to us. "Is this the first time you've seen
it?" the taller of the two asked.

"Yes, it is," I answered.

"You should try it sometime."

"Truth is," said Yaakov, "we wanted to ask if we could
borrow the ball to try it out."

The two looked at each other, and then the one who had
spoken said, "It's heavy. You have to pay attention to it or it
can hurt you."

"We'd be careful," said Yaakov.

"I don't see why you fellows can't have a try at it," the

second man said. "We'll show you where it's kept."

We thanked them, and they showed us a wooden box not far from where we were standing.

"You can take it from there and return it when you're finished," said the shorter man.

"But make sure there aren't people around who can get hurt," said the taller one.

"Or things that can get broken," the shorter one added.

"We'll be careful," I said, and we thanked them again.

We returned to the wooden box a little while later. Yaakov reached in to get the metal ball. "This is heavy," he said, managing to remove the ball with difficulty. He put the ball down on the deck, where it made a bang.

We faced each other at a short distance as we had seen the two ship's mates doing, and Yaakov rolled the heavy metal ball toward me. It rolled to the right, making it difficult for me to catch. I tried but failed to get a hold of the ball, which passed me to the side and smashed into the wall around the ship's deck.

"Does that mean that I won?" asked Yaakov.

"Of course not," I said. "You have to roll it to me, not somewhere off to the side."

I retrieved the ball and rolled it to Yaakov, who, after nearly missing it, actually did get the ball. He rolled it to me, and I caught it as well.

"I think we're getting the idea," Yaakov said.

We continued on in this way, with the heavy ball sometimes being caught by one of us and sometimes missing us and smashing into a wall.

It was Yaakov's turn to roll the ball. It lunged forward

at a quick pace, and it rolled past me, picking up speed as it moved. I turned to see it heading toward a wooden barrel at the far side of the deck.

The ball hit the barrel with force, and I was startled to see the wood crack from the impact. It was as if the barrel had exploded. Thick liquid that might have been oil flowed out onto the deck.

"Oh, what have I done!" Yaakov exclaimed.

That was when I heard a gravelly voice shout, "You've ruined valuable property, that's what you've done, you troublemaker!"

I turned to see the ship's captain standing there, his large eyes burning with anger.

"You'll pay for this," he growled to Yaakov. He called for his men to come and take care of the spilling oil. I hadn't liked this captain from the first moment I saw him, and I knew he was not going to be pleasant to deal with now.

Yaakov stood ashen-faced, as the men came to stem the oil spill. "Let's put the ball away, so at least those fellows who lent it to us won't be angry with us," I said, trying to distract him. We returned the ball to its box, and then slipped past the men working on the oil. The captain, thankfully, had left the scene.

"Maybe we should tell Rebbe Yitzchak about this," I said, and Yaakov nodded. We started toward Rebbe Yaakov's cabin, but never made it there. We heard the captain's voice behind us.

"You did a lot of damage, and now you'll come with me to work off what you owe."

We turned to face him.

"What exactly do you want him to do?" I asked.

"There's a cabin that needs cleaning."

"Well," I said, "let us get the rabbi. Perhaps he can pay the damages —"

"No," Yaakov said, interrupting me. "Why should Rebbe Yitzchak pay from either *tzedakah* money or his own pocket, if I can work off the debt without asking him for help?"

"I don't have all day to spend here while you argue among yourselves! If you're coming to do the work, then come!"

"Show me where to go," Yaakov said resignedly.

The captain gestured for Yaakov to come with him, and I followed.

They stopped in front of a door, which the captain threw open. "I want that room totally clean!" he yelled, and then stormed off.

We looked inside. He had called it a cabin, but it was much bigger than the other cabins. It was piled with discarded items. Cobwebs and dust filled every corner. Cleaning this cabin would be quite a job.

"We'd better get started," I said.

"We?"

"Oh, come now, don't tell me you plan to do this on your own."

"I did the damage —"

"We were playing the game together. Don't be silly, Yaakov. It could just as easily have happened when I was rolling the ball. Now let's go. The sooner we start, the sooner we finish."

He gave me a smile.

It took us hours to get that cabin into shape, but when

we finished, there was no way the captain would be able to claim we had not done our job. He wasn't happy about it, but when he came to inspect it, he could find nothing to criticize. Yaakov and I breathed a sigh of relief. We'd finished cleaning the cabin. More importantly though, we'd cemented our friendship.

CHAPTER TEN

After two weeks of traveling on the Mediterranean Sea, we reached the Italian city of Livorno. We were not allowed into the actual city. We had to stay in the Lazaretto — the quarantine station — like all visitors from the East, in order to prevent the spread of contagious diseases. We would stay there for a little over a month.

Shortly after our arrival, three baskets filled with food were delivered to us from the local Jewish community. They were much appreciated, especially after the scarcity of food on the ship because of the worms.

The Lazaretto was filled with people from many different places, in addition to those from Italy. Most were from the East so we could communicate easily, but we found that even communicating with the Italians wasn't that hard, especially those who were Jewish and knew some Hebrew.

From nearly the moment we arrived at the Lazaretto, Rebbe Yitzchak wrote intensely. It seemed to me that he was working on a *sefer*. When I asked him about it, he smiled and admitted that he was in fact working on a *sefer*.

"There is nowhere to go and nothing to do here. It is the perfect time to compose a *sefer*!" he said with a look in his eyes that I could not quite interpret. Before I knew it, though, he was back at his writing.

Being cooped up in a building for over a month can get a little boring. It was worse than being on the ship! Yaakov and I tried to explore as much as we could so that we wouldn't miss anything important.

On the third day of our stay in the Lazaretto, a strange character arrived from Tunisia. No one seemed to know his actual name but he called himself the "seer." He had a restless otherworldly appearance that I found unsettling. The truth is that some would describe Rebbe Yitzchak as having an otherworldly appearance as well, but believe me, they were very different. When you saw Rebbe Yitzchak, you felt calm. Although speaking to such a great person could make you feel a bit nervous, you still felt calm. With the "seer," it was different. When you saw him, you thought of chaos.

Word spread quickly throughout the Lazaretto that this man could see people's futures. Yaakov wanted to go and see what all the fuss was about.

"I don't know," I said.

"What's the problem?" he asked.

"I don't think Rebbe Yitzchak would approve of going to

this fellow. Who knows if his information comes from a pure source?"

"You mean you think he uses the forces of impurity?"

"Yaakov, I don't know, but I don't think we should get involved in it."

"All right, then let's just go and see what's happening there. We won't actually speak to him."

"I guess we could do that," I said.

We found people lined up to talk to the "seer." He sat on a large embroidered chair in a corner of a room. Where he had been able to find such a chair in the Lazaretto, I have no idea; maybe he'd brought it with him from Tunisia. We watched as one after another, people paid the man a substantial sum of money, and then spoke with him for a few minutes. When they'd finished, some looked bewildered, others looked worried, while others could not seem to stop smiling.

"Yaakov, I think we'd better go," I said, feeling more and more uneasy standing there. Yaakov was about to say something when we heard someone call out from the back of the room, "What do you say about Rabbi Yitzchak?"

The man looked up sharply from the woman he had been talking to. "Rabbi Yitzchak?"

"Yes," continued the fellow from the back of the room, "the rabbi from Israel who is now staying here in the Lazaretto."

The "seer" thought for a moment and then said, "I do not have anything to say about him." He was silent. A strange look came over his face for a moment, and then it was gone. "He has no need for my pronouncements." He then continued talking to the woman he had been speaking to before the interruption.

"What do you think of that?" Yaakov asked.

"I don't know exactly what to think of it," I said, "but I think it's time for us to go."

"All right," Yaakov agreed, and we began to head for the door. We were almost out of the room when a tall Arab man whom I recognized as a fellow passenger from the ship stopped us. "Aren't you going to ask him anything?"

"No," I said.

"Why not?"

"Listen," I said, "the future will be what it will be. What have we to ask?"

The Arab man laughed. "You sound almost like your rabbi already."

I took that as a compliment, and we left.

·   ☾

A few days later, my path and the path of the "seer" crossed. I was walking down the hall when I looked up and saw that he was walking toward me. He noticed me and stopped. He stared at me and then said, "You. Your father passed through this Lazaretto not long ago."

My heart jumped. He'd really taken me by surprise with that statement.

"But I dare not tell you any more, for the rabbi might not approve." He smiled, and it wasn't the type of smile that made you feel warm inside. Just then a fellow who looked a little older than me wearing the cap and uniform of the Lazaretto's employees passed by, and the man who called himself the seer seemed to lose interest in me. He continued on his way.

When I found Yaakov later, I told him of my encounter with the "seer."

"You think he knows where your father is?" he asked.

I shrugged. "If he does, he doesn't sound like he's going to tell, and I really don't think Rebbe Yitzchak would want me to talk to him."

"It must make you feel strange, though, hearing him mention your father like that."

"Very strange. On the one hand, it's comforting to know that he passed this way, but on the other hand, it's like getting a whiff of food when you're hungry and not being able to get the food."

He laughed at my comparison.

"Do you understand what I mean?"

"I do," he said, "but the food analogy still strikes me as funny."

"Speaking of food, I could use some about now, "I said.

"You won't get any argument from me about that."

We turned in the direction of the room where our food was stored, and I noticed a young man standing nearby. It took me a minute before I realized that this was the young Italian clerk I had just seen while talking with the "seer."

"I'm afraid I overheard you twice," he said, "but the first time was completely by accident."

"And what did you hear?" I asked.

"I heard that fellow who calls himself the 'seer' telling you that your father passed through here not long ago. And now I heard you implying that you don't know where your father is."

"So?"

"Is your father, by any chance, a man with a long black beard who walks with a slight limp, and who, in my humble opinion, you resemble quite strongly?"

I smiled at his words, but then I realized something. That must be why the "seer" made that comment to me. I look like my father.

"You've seen him?" I asked the clerk excitedly.

"I have."

"When?"

"As that so-called seer said, it was not long ago. I can't say exactly, but he left here no more than two weeks ago."

"He stayed here in the Lazaretto?"

"Yes, for several weeks."

"You don't know where he went from here?"

"I'm afraid not. I can't really tell you more than that 'seer' fellow already did, but at least I can tell you that I saw your father with my own eyes instead of giving you some mumbo jumbo. I can tell you that he seemed to be in good health and spirits."

"I really appreciate that. Could I ask your name?"

"Vitorio Rosini."

"I am Avraham Siman and this is Yaakov Agir."

"I am pleased to meet both of you, but I have to run now. I work here, you know." He smiled. "I hope to speak with you again during your stay in the Lazaretto."

"Be well," I said, "and thanks again for the 'regards' from my father. It means a lot to me."

He waved and hurried off.

When we related our experiences to Rebbe Yitzchak, he was happy we had not gotten more involved with the "seer."

"No good can come of it," he said.

"Rebbe, will I see my father again?"

"With the help of the Almighty, you will see your father and your mother and your sisters, and we will all be able to return to Eretz Yisrael."

"When will that be?"

"I don't know, Avraham, I don't know. But you know what I do know?"

"What?"

He pointed upwards. "There is One; no other."

CHAPTER ELEVEN

A little over a month after we arrived in Livorno and entered the Lazaretto, we were allowed to leave. We went immediately to the home of the well-known *baal tzedakah* Signor Michael Pereira, who welcomed us to stay as long as we wished. After we settled ourselves in the elegant house, Yaakov and I decided to explore the city. We'd been there over a month but had barely been outside. With the long stay in the Lazaretto coming right after the two-month journey at sea, both of us were eager to get out and do some exploring. When I told Rebbe Yitzchak that we were going, he nodded his head in approval.

"You have to get out a little," he commented. "It's healthy for you."

As we left the house, Yaakov told me something that made

me wonder. "Avraham, you know that *sefer* Rebbe Yitzchak was working on in the Lazaretto?"

"Yes."

"He finished it before we left the Lazaretto."

"He wrote an entire *sefer* while in the Lazaretto?"

"Yes."

"I wonder what it's about."

"So do I."

"But how do you know that he finished it, Yaakov?"

"I overheard Rebbe Yitzchak telling Signor Pereira."

"Are you serious?"

"Would I make this up?"

"A whole *sefer* while in the Lazaretto? Very interesting. He *was* writing a lot when we were there."

"Yes, he was. But I have something even more interesting to tell you."

"What?"

"I also overheard something strange about this *sefer*."

"Tell me."

"Rebbe Yitzchak said something about this *sefer* having to do with you."

"Me?"

"Yes, he said something like, 'This *sefer* is on account of Avraham.'"

"What does that mean?"

"I have no idea."

"You think the *sefer* has something to do with this Abu Rash fellow who's chasing my father and me?"

"What would a *sefer* have to do with that?"

"That's what I'm asking you."

"You don't want to ask Rebbe Yitzchak about it, do you?"

"No, I wouldn't feel comfortable doing that," I said with a smile. "Especially since I'd have to tell him that you were eavesdropping on his conversation with Signor Pereira."

Yaakov laughed. I thought about what he'd told me and wondered if and when I'd find out what Rebbe Yitzchak had meant with his strange words.

We decided to walk through the city and see what we could find of interest. I knew a little about the city and its history from Uncle Gavriel, and as we walked I related what I knew.

"Livorno, also known as Leghorn, is the main port of the Tuscany region in central Italy," I said.

Yaakov laughed. "Avraham, you sound like those missionaries who keep coming to Yerushalayim."

"How so?"

"They also sound like they're reading from a script."

"Well, if you want me to stop ..."

"Not at all, Avraham. It's interesting. Go ahead."

"Well, the Jews of the city specialize in the working of coral, which they export as far as Russia and India."

"I guess they have access to coral since they live near the water."

"Yes. They're also involved in the manufacture of soap and paper."

"So I guess they make nice livings."

"Well, when Tuscany recently became part of the larger Kingdom of Italy, the city became less important as a port since other ports are now competing with it."

"I've seen *sefarim* that were printed here."

"Yes, Livorno is a center of Hebrew printing."

"What about the Haskalah we hear about that is weakening people's *emunah* and observance of mitzvos in many parts of Europe? Has it come to Italy as well?"

"Unfortunately, it has. There has been a lessening in the careful observance of mitzvos among some Jews here. The recent granting of equal rights to Jews in Tuscany has also contributed to this. It seems that when we can be more free, it gives some people the feeling that they can be free of Hashem as well."

"Can Jews really live as they want to in Italy?"

"Officially, yes, but it also depends on where. You must have heard about the Mortara case that is causing such an uproar around the world."

"The little boy?"

"Yes. Edgardo Mortara, a six-year-old Jewish boy living in the Italian city of Bologna, was kidnapped several years ago by the church police to be raised as a Catholic."

"Will they return him?"

"His parents are trying their best to get him back, but the church is not giving in."

"It reminds me of that boy from Eretz Yisrael who seems to have been taken away by the Greek Orthodox priests from Yerushalayim."

"Well, here in Italy it's the Catholic Church we're talking about rather than the Greek Orthodox Church, but I see what you mean."

We were silent for a moment, and then Yaakov said, "Tell me the truth, Avraham. How many of the fellows in your yeshivah back in Eretz Yisrael would have all this information?"

I smiled. "Not too many, but they don't have an Uncle Gavriel — at least not my Uncle Gavriel."

We had been touring the city for about half an hour when we heard a commotion on the next street. We followed the noise and saw a group of people watching two Italian policemen who were putting handcuffs on a man's hands. While the man didn't seem to be putting up much of a physical struggle, he was making quite a verbal protest at his arrest.

"Avraham, it's that 'seer' fellow from the Lazaretto!"

I could see that Yaakov was in fact correct. The "seer" now wore a turban, but it was clearly him.

Yaakov went over to one of the onlookers. "What's happening here?" he asked.

"He's some sort of fortune teller."

"Is that illegal here?"

The onlooker laughed. "Not as far as I know, but it seems this fellow has been charging exorbitant prices for his services, and the police say that he's a liar and a faker."

Yaakov thanked the man for his time and we watched as the two policemen started moving the "seer" forward toward a waiting police wagon.

As they passed us, the "seer" noticed me. His eyes widened and he stopped in his tracks.

"You! You aren't who I thought you were, are you?"

I said nothing. I could feel the eyes of the crowd watching me.

"When you are on the side of evil, you can become part of it!"

A chill swept through me when he uttered these words. Just then, one of the policemen gave the "seer" a push.

"Why are you giving free advice all of a sudden?" he asked snidely.

"Yes," his partner added, "you usually charge good money for this."

They continued to hustle the "seer" toward the police wagon. Suddenly, he turned around and looked at me, his wild eyes open so wide that they seemed to be straining at their sockets.

"Evil!" he shrieked.

Again I felt a chill run through me.

"That will be enough, Signor," one of the policemen said as he and his partner hoisted him up onto the wagon.

We watched the wagon drive off while several people looked at me. One old woman came over and said, "Don't pay him any mind, young man. He's obviously crazy. Screaming loudly doesn't make something true."

I smiled weakly at her.

"What he says means nothing," she said, and then walked off.

I knew she was probably right, but for some reason that didn't take away the chill I still felt.

It must have shown on my face because Yaakov asked, "Avraham, is everything all right?"

I looked at him. After a moment of silence, I finally answered him.

"I hope so."

I don't really know why the words of the "seer" had so disturbed me; it actually took several minutes until I was myself again. Yaakov tried to distract me, and we continued our walk through Livorno. Eventually I became absorbed in what we were talking about and the incident slowly receded from my mind. But the rest of our walk was not destined to pass in peace.

I noticed that Yaakov seemed to be paying little attention to what I was saying. He also seemed to be furtively trying to get a look at something.

"Yaakov, what's happening?"

"Listen, Avraham. Very slowly, I am going to turn slightly and you are going to turn to face me."

"I am?"

"You will make it seem as if we are involved in an intense conversation."

"Yaakov, what —"

"Then you will very carefully take a look at the fellow across the street several yards behind us, wearing the black *keffiyeh*-type headdress. Not yet!"

"All right," I said, somewhat embarrassed that I had not followed his instructions.

"Wait till I turn, so it won't look like you're turning to look at him."

"I'll try."

"When you do, you'll be able to tell me if he's the one you ran into at the mosque back in Alexandria."

Slowly, Yaakov turned, and I turned to face him. Ever so carefully, I looked across the street as I blabbered to Yaakov as if we were discussing the fate of the world.

"I see who you mean. No, it's not him."

"You're sure?"

"I'm sure, Yaakov, but why did you ask?"

"I think he's been following us."

"Really?" I felt a stab of fear.

"I can't be sure, but I think so."

We continued walking. When Yaakov stole another glance, he saw that the man was still across the street and still several yards back.

"How can we know for sure if he's following us?" Yaakov asked.

"Listen to me, Yaakov. Do you see that carriage and the horses stopped on the next street?"

"Yes, I see them."

"I'm going to duck out of sight behind them, and at the same time you are going to cross the street. Let's see what he does when we split up."

"It's worth a try."

As we passed the carriage, I dove under it. Once underneath it, I looked out and saw Yaakov cross the street and then keep on walking. Not far behind him, I saw the man in the black *keffiyeh*. He seemed confused as he looked in my general direction. Then he looked at Yaakov and continued walking. I crept out from underneath the carriage and started walking slowly on my side of the street behind the man and Yaakov.

We all walked for a few minutes in this strange procession. Then Yaakov turned a corner and I waited to see if the man with the black *keffiyeh* would turn as well. He did. I, too, turned the corner. A moment later, Yaakov stopped. The man with the *keffiyeh* stopped as well, and so did I.

I figured this had gone on long enough. I walked a little faster, passing the man with the black *keffiyeh* walking across the street from me. I crossed the street and joined Yaakov.

"There's no question about it, Yaakov."

"He's following us?"

"Yes, he is."

"What now?"

"We lose him."

"How?"

A carriage was passing. It gave me an idea.

"You see the ledge on the back of that carriage?"

"Yes. You think we can jump on?"

"That's what I'm wondering."

We walked faster to keep up with the carriage.

"Are you ready, Avraham?"

I took a deep breath. "I guess so ...."

"It was your idea," he said, and smiled.

We ran toward the carriage and jumped. I found myself standing on the ledge of the moving carriage, but I felt that I was about to fall off. I had to find something to hold on to. I flailed about trying to keep my balance as the carriage moved forward.

"Above you, Avraham!"

I looked up as one part of my brain registered that Yaakov, too, had made it and was standing on the carriage ledge beside me.

"Grab the post above you!"

I saw the post he meant. It was a thin metal rod running along the top of the carriage. I grabbed for it, and with help from Above got a hold of it. I don't think I could have kept my balance for another second.

My heart beating fast, I looked at Yaakov. He, too, was holding on to the metal post.

"Did we lose him?" I asked, trying to cover the quiver in my voice.

I saw Yaakov turning to look behind us. "I don't see our man anywhere," he said. "I think we did it."

"Now we just have to get off this thing."

Just then the carriage came to a stop.

A man who was apparently the driver came around to the back of the carriage. He didn't look happy. "I thought I felt something on the back of the carriage."

Yaakov and I jumped down.

"Young people. I'll never understand them," the driver said as he waved his hands in disgust and walked away.

"Let's find our way back to Signor Pereira's house," Yaakov suggested.

I nodded in agreement.

We walked in silence at first, each of us lost in thought. It was Yaakov who broke the silence. "He has to be one of Abu Rash's men. Who else could he be?"

"Sounds right to me."

"These people really mean business. They're not just joking around."

"It seems so. Can you tell me how they knew we went to Livorno?"

"I have no idea."

"But even if they somehow knew, I would never have imagined they would follow us here."

"As I said, Avraham, these fellows are not playing games. This is serious business to them."

"And these guys are after my father, and me, too. Not a very comforting thought."

Yaakov said nothing.

"You know, since that run-in I had with that fellow at the mosque in Alexandria, there's something I've been wondering about. Did he actually realize that I was my father's son, or was he just after me because he recognized me as someone who'd been with Rebbe Yitzchak?"

"And what do you think now?"

"I still don't know. I mean, if they're going to the trouble of following us to Italy, they must at least suspect that Rebbe Yitzchak got something past them."

"You mean it's not likely that they're going to such efforts just because Rebbe Yitzchak didn't stop to chat with them back there in the desert."

"Right. I mean, I don't know for sure if they know that I — Avraham Siman — am here, but they suspect something."

"I've told you this before, Avraham, but I'll say it again: That Abu Rash is *not* my favorite person."

"Well, he and his thugs are not making a friend out of me either."

We continued on in silence as we made our way back to the Pereira house.

Later, I went over to Rebbe Yitzchak. He had heard about our adventure with the man wearing the black *keffiyeh*, and asked how I was.

"I'm fine, Rebbe, but something is bothering me."

"What is it, Avraham?"

"If Abu Rash is interested in following us and is able to follow us, then it's very likely he would be interested in and able to follow my father as well."

Rabbi Yitzchak was silent.

"I'm scared for him."

"What you are saying is not unreasonable, Avraham, but keep in mind that your father had a head start on them. He left before they realized what was happening. I hope that will give him an advantage. Meanwhile, it seems that someone is definitely after us, and while we should not be afraid, we should act with caution."

"I hope this whole affair will end up all right, Rebbe."

"I feel that it will, Avraham."

I then told Rebbe Yitzchak about our encounter with the "seer." I was still upset about what the "seer" had said to me.

He frowned. "As we have discussed, Avraham, the less one has to do with that sort of person, the better."

"I know, Rebbe, but in the Lazaretto people seemed to think that he knew things about them."

"People are easily fooled, Avraham. It is better to have nothing to do with him. These "seer" types are just clever tricksters who know how to convince people of things and try to make money from it."

"Rebbe would not believe how many people were ready to pay him to hear what he had to say."

He smiled sadly. "I'm afraid I would believe it, Avraham. I've been around a while, you know."

"Why are people so drawn to such things, Rebbe?"

"People have within them an innate sense of *emunah*. They are born with a feeling of faith and belief. If that feeling is not directed where it should be, it goes in other directions. Wise people believe in the Almighty. Others put their power of belief into people like this 'seer' or into false ideologies."

"Rebbe, he said that when one is on the side of evil, one can become part of it. That is true, isn't it?"

"Avraham, you didn't need that fellow to tell you that, did you?"

I smiled.

"Avraham, if you take my advice, you won't give what he said any more thought."

"But, Rebbe —"

Rebbe Yitzchak looked at me for a moment and then said, "Avraham, if I did not like you as much as I do, I might be tempted to get a little annoyed with you."

I laughed.

"I think that too much of your valuable time has already been taken up with this man's words."

I thanked Rebbe Yitzchak and left his room feeling much calmer than I'd felt before, but I could not shake the feeling that there were more surprises in store for us.

CHAPTER TWELVE

J saw a man sitting at a table. His back was to me and I could not see his face. The room was dark, very dark. It was so dark that I was surprised I could see. A voice said, "That's your father, Avraham." I looked at the figure and wondered how that could be my father; even from the back I could tell that it was not my father.

I came closer to the man and tapped him on the shoulder. He turned, and to my horror I saw that he had no face. His face was darkness. "He is the king of the dark side, and you are the prince," said the same voice. I realized that the voice belonged to the "seer."

I knew that I was dreaming, and yet I felt captive to the world of the dream.

"Who are you?" I demanded of the man.

"I am the dark that is in all mankind."

"And what have you to do with me?"

"I am the king, and you are the prince."

I could not look at the man's face. It frightened me too much.

A door opened and in walked Rebbe Yitzchak. Wherever he went, it was light.

"There can be light in the darkness," said the man at the table, "but the darkness is still there. It can engulf you."

"Not if you choose not to let it engulf you," Rebbe Yitzchak countered.

"Rebbe, can I come to stand near you? I am afraid of the darkness."

"Avraham, there is no darkness. It only looks like darkness. Banish it and it will disappear."

"I don't know how, Rebbe."

"You do, Avraham. Every word of Torah, every mitzvah, every act of kindness is light. You are filled with light."

The man at the table screamed, "He is not! He is darkness. He is the prince of the dark!"

Rebbe Yitzchak walked slowly toward the man.

"No! Stop now!" the man shouted. "Stay away from me!"

"Do you fear the truth?"

"I fear the light!"

There was a knock on the door. I looked up and saw Rebbe Yekusiel of Tzefas in the doorway.

"Why is everyone arguing?" he wanted to know.

"Who is arguing?" my sister Tziporah asked.

"Tziporah, what are you doing here?" I wondered aloud.

"What are *you* doing here, Avraham?"

"Where is Sarah?"

"Where do you think she is?"

"Why do you answer my questions with more questions?"

Then she was gone. I looked for Rebbe Yekusiel, but he, too, was gone. It didn't matter, as long as Rebbe Yitzchak was there. But when I looked for him, I couldn't find him either.

"It's just you and me now, son."

I looked at the man with darkness for a face and said, "Don't you call me son."

"Don't be afraid of me."

"Why should I be afraid of you? This is only a dream."

He got up from the table and started to move in my direction. I felt very afraid.

"There is nothing to fear," my mother said.

But then she, too, was gone, and the man with no face continued to advance toward me.

I was very alone and very scared. I started to cry. "Stay away from me!"

"What is it, Avraham?" Yaakov asked. "Are you all right?"

Was Yaakov here as well?

"Avraham, are you all right?"

I opened my eyes. Yaakov was standing there looking worried. "You must have been having *some* dream, Avraham."

He was certainly right about that.

"How are you now?"

"I'm fine. That was definitely the strangest dream I can ever remember having. I knew I was dreaming, but it didn't help."

"It had to do with what that 'seer' fellow said, didn't it?"

"Why do you say that?"

"You spoke in your sleep, and that's what it sounded like."

"Sorry for waking you up."

"That crazy fellow really spooked you."

"I guess he did. I suppose that he, and the whole situation, are getting to me."

"I can understand that."

"As I said, I'm sorry I woke you."

"You didn't wake me."

"You just happened to be up in the middle of the night?"

"That's right. How loudly do you think you were talking in your sleep?"

"How would I know?"

"Well, it wasn't loud enough to wake me from a deep sleep. I was up already."

"Something bothering you, too?"

Yaakov laughed. "I guess so."

"Yaakov?"

"Yes?"

"Do you think there's bad in every person?"

"Avraham, it's past midnight and you want to discuss deep things?"

"You said you weren't sleepy."

"I didn't say that."

"So what did you say?"

"I said I couldn't sleep. That doesn't mean it's the middle of the day and I'm all alert."

"All right."

"Why do you ask?"

"About what?"

"About if there's bad in everyone."

"Something in my dream. I heard someone saying, *I am the dark that is in all mankind.*"

"Oh, wow, you really did have some dream."

"It was a strange one, all right."

"I mean, everyone has a *yetzer hara*, don't they?"

"We can always choose good. That's basically what Rebbe Yitzchak said in the dream."

"What did you eat for supper? Do you always have such heavy dreams?"

I laughed at Yaakov's words, and it felt good to laugh. For the first time since I'd woken, I began to feel a little calmer.

"I had the same thing for supper as you did, Yaakov — Signora Pereira's famous broiled chicken and potatoes."

"I hope that doesn't mean I'm also going to dream about the fight between good and evil."

"Maybe it depends on how much you ate."

We bantered on for another few minutes until Yaakov started yawning. "It's been great chatting, but maybe it would be an idea to try to get some sleep, no?"

I was afraid to go back to sleep. I didn't want to meet the man with no face again. I was annoyed with myself for being afraid, but I couldn't help it.

Somehow Yaakov must have understood what I was thinking because he said, "Listen, if I notice you having another nightmare like that, I'll be sure to wake you up. All right?"

I was really touched that he'd understood and made the offer. "Thanks," I said.

It was good to have a friend.

We weren't sure how long we would stay in Livorno. Rebbe Yitzchak visited those individuals who were involved in gathering funds for the communities of Eretz Yisrael, as he did on all his trips. Rebbe Yitzchak was not a *shaliach* for Eretz Yisrael in the way that *shluchim* had been in years past, like when the holy Chida traveled as a *shaliach*. Nowadays, especially in Western Europe, the Jewish communities didn't want individual emissaries coming from the holy land to collect funds. Instead, a central organization had been set up in Amsterdam known as the *Pekidei u'Mashgichei v'Amarkelei Eretz Yisrael* (officers, overseers and treasurers of Eretz Yisrael), where donations from throughout Western Europe would be gathered and sent to Eretz Yisrael.

Rebbe Yitzchak's missions were not actually to collect funds but to see to it that things were running smoothly and to encourage people to donate generously to the central fund. He went around Livorno doing this, but I had a feeling that something else was keeping him in the city. As in Alexandria, he used the telegraph office on several occasions. Again, I did not ask why.

After a few days had passed, both Yaakov and I wanted to go out exploring again. Despite the fact that we knew there was someone in town looking for us, we simply felt too cooped up to stay in the Pereira home all day long.

When we asked Rebbe Yitzchak if we could leave the house, he agreed. "You need to get out," he said, "but please be cautious."

As we walked along the streets of Livorno for the second

time since we'd arrived, I decided that this might be a good time to ask Yaakov about his story. I knew I was taking a chance, since he'd only opened up to me recently, but I acted on emotion instead of logic.

"Yaakov?"

"Yes?"

"What did Abu Rash do to you?"

"What do you mean?"

"You've mentioned several times how you feel about Abu Rash and his gang. What made you feel this way?"

"I see that you don't only like to ask heavy questions in the middle of the night after you've had a crazy dream," Yaakov retorted dryly. "You'll do it in the middle of the day as well."

I laughed, but said nothing. My question hung in the air.

He was silent for a moment, and then said, "He made your father go away, didn't he?"

"He definitely did."

"Well, mine, too."

"Your father had to go away, too?"

"Yes. Forever."

It took a second for this to sink in, and then I slowly asked, "You mean ..."

"Yes. He's no longer living."

"I'm sorry. I shouldn't have asked about —"

"It's all right. Maybe it's good to talk."

I said nothing, and then he continued, "We lived in the north, where Abu Rash started his gang. One of the things he does is find people who are in desperate need of money and lend it to them. He ends up making money on the deal, and if the unfortunate person can't pay back, even better."

"Better?"

"Yes, because then that person pretty much becomes Abu Rash's slave. That's what happened to my father. He couldn't repay the loan when Abu Rash demanded payment, so they took him to Izmir, Turkey, to work off the debt."

"Why Turkey?"

"Although the north of Eretz Yisrael is the center of the gang's activities, it seems that their second most important base of operations is in Turkey. When that captain on the ship demanded that I work off my debt, I thought to myself, *Like father, like son*. But you helped me out then, and I really appreciate it."

I made a motion that I hoped communicated my feelings that anyone else would have done the same.

"After a few weeks," he continued, "we got a note from a *rav* in Turkey saying that my father had died."

"What happened?"

"We don't know. My father was not a very strong person. Perhaps it was too much for him. The truth is we just don't know."

"I'm really sorry to hear this."

"Now you know why I dislike Abu Rash."

"Yes. I thought Rebbe Yitzchak had asked you to come along just to help out, but in truth, he had more in mind. We are both victims of Abu Rash, and I think he felt it made sense for both of us to be here in this battle against him."

"Avraham, you're right. But it's even more than that."

"What do you mean?"

"You're on this journey to stay out of the clutches of Abu Rash."

"Yes?"

"But that's not your only goal, is it?"

"What are you saying, Yaakov?"

"Deep down you want to find your father somewhere during this trip."

I didn't respond. I couldn't. He had spoken the truth. It was what I dreamed about at night.

"Am I right, Avraham?"

"Yes, Yaakov, you are."

Before we left Eretz Yisrael, my friend Moshe had said the same thing. I hadn't minded then, and somehow, when Yaakov said it, I didn't mind either.

"You're looking for your father, Avraham, and so am I."

When I looked at him with a question in my eyes, he said, "We have a good idea of where my father is buried in Turkey. I am going to find his grave. I want to visit my father's *kever*. My father was a simple Jew, not a great man or a hero, but he was a good man, and he was my father, and he deserves to have his grave visited by a relative. That is why Rebbe Yitzchak took me along."

I felt a powerful bond of friendship with Yaakov at that moment, a bond of suffering. I also felt a sense of wonder toward Rebbe Yitzchak, a man who seemed to never leave the four *amos* of *halachah*, and yet was able to be so aware of the needs and feelings of others.

Yaakov looked at me hesitantly and then said, "Avraham, I hope you won't be offended by this question, but could I ask how things are between you and your father?"

"What do you mean?"

"Well, since my father has been gone, I've started noticing

how boys my age get along with their fathers."

"So what have you noticed?"

"It depends. Some get along better than others. I had a pretty good relationship with my father, but now that he's gone, I really wish I'd paid more attention to some of the things he used to tell me."

"Well, *baruch Hashem*, I also get along pretty well with my father," I said.

"There's nothing you would do differently when you find him?"

At first I was offended by this, but then I looked into Yaakov's eyes and saw no spite, only sadness. "I don't know about changing anything, although I'm sure my *kibud av* could use improvement. But honestly, there is one thing that bothers me a lot."

Yaakov looked at me. "Yes?"

"I'm afraid that I'll never measure up to what my father expects of me. He's never expressed disappointment in my learning, but I know that he expects me to become a *talmid chacham* like he is. I really don't want to disappoint him, and I'm afraid I will."

"You like to learn, I can see that. So why are you so worried?"

"Yes, I learn, but I'm not sure I could ever be like him. I just don't know if I could spend every moment learning."

"How long has this been bothering you?"

"A long time. But since my father left, I've really begun to think about it a lot."

"Yes, it's funny how when you lose something, you start thinking about it more."

What Yaakov said made sense to me. When I'd had daily contact with my father, I pushed my concerns to the back of my mind, but somehow my father's leaving had brought these feelings to the surface. It's as if not talking to him had forced me to think about him more, and thinking about my father had made me focus on my fears regarding his hopes for me.

Yaakov pulled me out of my reverie by asking, "Have you spoken to Rebbe Yitzchak about this?"

"I did."

"And what did he say?"

"He told me not to worry." I smiled sheepishly. "But deep down I still worry."

Yaakov nodded sympathetically.

I'm not sure where the discussion would have gone if something hadn't caught Yaakov's eye. Our conversation came to a sudden halt.

"Avraham!"

"What is it?"

"Does that man in front of us look at all familiar to you?"

He certainly did look familiar to me. It was our friend with the black *keffiyeh*.

"What should we do now?" I asked nervously.

"Return the favor."

"What?"

"The other day he followed us, so today we follow him."

We slowed down so that we'd be farther behind him. He carried a basket that seemed to be filled with food.

"You never know where these fellows will turn up next," Yaakov remarked. "One day following two fellows from the holy land, the next day delivering food packages to the poor."

I smiled. "It looks like the *mishlo'ach manos* baskets my aunt prepares each Purim."

Yaakov laughed. "Yes. Happy Purim from Abu Rash."

Suddenly, the man turned into a market. We stopped at a distance to wait for him to come out. Several minutes passed, but he did not emerge.

"Don't tell me he slipped away like I did from the fellow in the mosque in Alexandria," I said in exasperation.

"If he did, that means he noticed us," Yaakov said.

"How could he have noticed us? I don't understand."

"Personally, I don't think he did, Avraham. Maybe he's just taking his time buying his *mishlo'ach manos.*"

I didn't think it was so funny, because there was no way he could have realized we were trailing him. These people weren't magicians, were they?

"Happy Purim," Yaakov said suddenly and pointed. I looked and saw our man emerging from the market with his basket even more full than before.

"He's making me hungry with all that food," I said, as we continued to follow from a safe distance.

After we'd been trailing the fellow with the black *keffiyeh* for about ten minutes, Yaakov asked, "Doesn't this neighborhood look familiar to you?"

I'd been thinking the same thing. Then I realized that we were not far from the Lazaretto. When I mentioned this to Yaakov, he agreed that we were in fact quite close to the Lazaretto. After another minute of walking, the Lazaretto came into view. We were taken aback to see the man enter the building.

"What's he doing in the Lazaretto?" Yaakov wondered aloud.

"You think we should sneak in to the delivery entrance and try to see what he's up to?" I asked. After all, we knew our way around the building and its various entrances.

"Sounds like a good idea to me."

We turned the corner, and after looking around carefully, we entered the small delivery entrance. There was no one around in the receiving area, so we quietly moved farther into the building. We found people standing around, but no one gave us a second glance. So many different people passed through this building that we drew no attention at all. We continued on, trying to stay in the shadows as best as we could.

It was when we entered a sitting room on the second floor that we saw our man. He was talking to another man, who was holding the care package that "black *keffiyeh*" had been carrying. The two were involved in an intense conversation and did not notice us. We, however, could see them clearly, and there was no doubt that the man "black *keffiyeh*" was speaking with was the fellow I had escaped from at the mosque in Alexandria.

CHAPTER THIRTEEN

Without communicating with each other, Yaakov and I both started to slowly back out of the doorway we had just entered. Neither of us wanted to meet these two men at such close quarters. While they would probably be limited in what they could do inside the Lazaretto, I didn't feel like taking any chances; neither, apparently, did Yaakov.

I breathed a sigh of relief as we exited the room. We went down the stairs backwards, so that our backs would not be facing Abu Rash's men if they came out of the room. We did not want any more surprises. Leaving the building, we crossed the street where we could stand at a safe distance and decide what to do next.

I looked at Yaakov. "You were right. This isn't a game; they're serious about this."

"He must have recently arrived from Eretz Yisrael and is putting in the required time at the Lazaretto."

"Yes, and his fellow gangster is bringing him *mishlo'ach manos*."

Despite the serious look on his face, Yaakov gave a little laugh. "Happy Purim."

"It doesn't seem that Abu Rash is going to stop at anything."

"He never does, Avraham."

Just then we saw "black *keffiyeh*" emerge from the Lazaretto.

"Do we follow him again?" I asked.

"We try."

But almost immediately the man boarded a carriage.

"Are you in the mood for another ride on a carriage ledge?" Yaakov asked.

"If I don't think about it too much."

We ran to the carriage and stepped up on the ledge just as it started to move. This time, I held on tightly to the top post. The carriage began to pick up speed but then slowed down as a loud voice bellowed for it to stop. From behind the carriage, a policeman was running straight toward us.

"Maybe," I said nervously, "this wasn't such a good idea."

The carriage came to a halt just as the policeman reached our side. "What on earth are you two doing?" he demanded.

"Getting a ride," Yaakov answered.

"Did you pay for a ride?"

"No, sir," he said.

"Then get off. Now!"

We did.

"If I ever see you two doing something like that again, I'll have you jailed. Is that clear?"

We both confirmed that it was very clear.

"Now get out of here!"

He went to the front of the carriage to tell the driver that he could proceed, and we walked off.

"Nice show, fellows," said a nearby voice. I looked up and saw Vitorio Rosini smiling at us. He was wearing a sporty grey cap.

"Do you remember me?" he asked.

"Sure we do," Yaakov said. "You're the fellow who works in the Lazaretto, and who saw Avraham's father."

"You fellows put on quite a show there. You're lucky he didn't arrest you and put you in jail overnight."

"Glad you enjoyed it," said Yaakov.

"Tell me, Vitorio," I said, "have you seen a newcomer from the holy land in the Lazaretto? He's an Arab man —"

"And he was talking to the fellow who was in the carriage you jumped on. Is that the one you mean?"

"Yes, it is."

"I've seen him, certainly."

"When did he arrive?" Yaakov asked.

"A few days ago. Why? Do you know him?"

"Not really," I said, "but we like to keep up with our fellow countrymen when they come to Italy. It's interesting for us."

"I see," he said, but he didn't seem to believe me.

"Should I tell him that you fellows were asking about him?"

"No, he wouldn't know us," I said.

"But I can tell him that some of his fellow countrymen were interested in him."

"Better not to," Yaakov said hastily.

"Why not?"

"What good could come of it?" Yaakov asked.

"Well, if you fellows specifically do not want me to tell him that you were asking about him, I won't."

"So, is the Lazaretto crowded these days?" Yaakov asked, obviously trying to change the subject.

"It's about the same as it was when you fellows were there. Of course, many of the people are different, but the number of people is about the same. And there is one major difference from when you were there."

"Oh, and what is that?" I asked.

"Well, it should be obvious."

"It's not obvious to me," Yaakov countered.

"Your friend. Your countryman, as you call him — he's the major difference."

"Why is he such a major difference?" Yaakov asked.

"You tell me."

I was getting a little nervous. Vitorio was toying with us. He seemed to know something that we didn't know. I was angry with myself for having brought up the subject of the Arab newcomer. On the other hand, Vitorio had impressed me as a good person, and I'm usually a good judge of character.

"Listen, Vitorio," Yaakov said, "what is it about that Arab fellow? Why are you so curious about him?"

"It was Avraham who seemed curious about him. I am simply wondering why."

Yaakov and I were both silent. Neither of us knew what to say. Vitorio smiled. "Listen, I'm on your side. You can relax." He removed his cap, pulled a *kippah* from his pocket and put it on his head. It looked very natural there.

"I know that in Eretz Yisrael, this would be unusual, but here there are *shomrei Torah u'mitzvos* who do not wear a *kippah* when going among the nations. You should know, though, that I have not eaten or said a *tefillah* or learned *Gemara* without a head covering since I was three years old. Not once."

Like I said, I'm a good judge of character.

"You study *Gemara*?" Yaakov asked.

"Yes, of course."

"In a yeshivah?" I asked.

"There are some institutions for Jewish learning here, but my father would rather I study with private tutors."

"You learn at home with them?" asked Yaakov.

"Sometimes we do, and sometimes we study in a local *beis kenesses*."

"What are you learning?" I asked.

"Bava Metzia."

"Which *perek*?"

"Why, Yaakov, do you wish to test me?" he asked with an eager smile. "You want to see if I am really who I say I am and not some imposter, or one of those Jews from the Haskalah who know more of Italian culture than about *perek Eilu Metzios*?"

"*Eilu Metzios*?" I repeated.

"Yes," Vitorio confirmed. "That is the *perek* I am learning."

"If I found an object on a street like this in my hometown near Yerushalayim, could I keep it?" Yaakov asked.

"It depends what that object was," Vitorio answered.

"An apple," I offered.

"You could keep it."

"Why?" Yaakov asked.

"There's no *siman*. Come on, you fellows from Eretz Yisrael should be able to come up with better than that."

"If someone lost an item that has no *siman*, but didn't yet realize that he'd lost it, can the finder keep it?" I asked.

"Avraham, do you want me to decide between Abaye and Rava?"

"Well, whose opinion is accepted according to the *halachah*?" Yaakov queried.

"The *halachah* is according to Abaye."

"Now I have a strong question for you, Vitorio."

"Yes, Avraham?"

"Why did you not tell us all this when we first met you?"

"That's a good question. You have to understand that I was in a rush. I also did not feel that it was the right place to get into lengthy discussions."

"You scared me there for a second, Vitorio, asking us all those questions about the Arab fellow," I said.

"Well, I really want to know what your connection to him is. I'm not asking for details, because I get the feeling that this is something better not discussed openly, but I do want to know what I should look out for. I work here every day and I can keep my eyes on him."

"We really appreciate your help," I said.

"It's the least I can do. I know you are traveling with the *tzaddik* who was staying here, and I'm sure that he is involved in this."

"He is," Yaakov said.

"Then it is my privilege to do what I can to help."

"Have you noticed anything about this fellow that was out of the ordinary?" I asked.

"He must have some sort of influence, because as you know, the people who run the Lazaretto are pretty strict about limiting contact between people inside and the people outside. Even I am limited as to where I can go and for how long. Yet, as you saw, he was able to have a conversation for several minutes with the other Arab fellow."

"What type of influence do you think he might have?" Yaakov asked.

"I don't know, perhaps money."

"You mean he or someone working with him might have bribed someone at the Lazaretto?"

"Possibly, Avraham. I don't know. Tell me what I should be on the lookout for."

"You can see if he has any other visitors," said Yaakov. "What else can you think of, Avraham?"

"Try to notice if he does anything suspicious, I suppose."

"I'll keep my eyes open. Tell me where you're staying in case I have something of importance to tell."

"At the home of Signor Michael Pereira," I said.

"Ah, yes, I know that home."

"I suppose that our friend will be staying in the Lazaretto about as long as we did?"

"Yes, Avraham. Since he came from the same country, he will stay about a month."

Vitorio carefully took off his *kippah* and put it way. "I hope we will meet again."

We shook hands with him and then he was off to the Lazaretto.

Yaakov and I began to walk in the opposite direction when I noticed that my shoe was untied.

"Just a minute, Yaakov. Let me take care of this." I walked a few yards away to where a bench stood. I put my foot on it and tied my shoe. It was an act I'd done so many times before; I could probably do it in my sleep. It took less than half a minute.

When I'd finished, Yaakov was nowhere to be found. I looked around the street but could not find him. At first I thought he was playing a joke on me. After ten minutes of wandering the area, I was sure that it was no joke. With fear rising in me, I looked for the policeman we had seen earlier, but could not find him. I described Yaakov as best I could in broken Italian to several bystanders. No one had seen him.

Yaakov was gone.

CHAPTER FOURTEEN

J didn't know what to do. I was in shock. I could not accept the fact that one moment Yaakov was there and the next moment he was gone. What had happened? Had Abu Rash's men grabbed him? I shuddered at the thought. What could I do? I thought for a moment of running back to let Rebbe Yitzchak know what was going on, but then remembered that Vitorio was right inside the Lazaretto. Perhaps he could help.

I snuck in the same entrance Yaakov and I had crept in not long before. I prayed that I would find Vitorio before I bumped into Lazaretto officials or Abu Rash's man. Hashem was with me and I found him almost immediately after I entered the building.

"What is it, Avraham?"

"Yaakov has disappeared."

"Disappeared?"

I described everything that had happened from the moment Vitorio had gone back to the Lazaretto until I realized that Yaakov was missing.

"No one saw anything?"

"There was no one around in the immediate vicinity. When I asked people who were nearby, they knew nothing." As I recounted what had happened, I became even more nervous. I was afraid for Yaakov, and to be honest, for myself as well. How were these people able to simply grab someone from thin air?

"Vitorio, what will we do?" I asked frantically.

"Give me a moment, Avraham." He seemed to be thinking. "Avraham," he finally said, "I want you to go back outside of the Lazaretto, but wait near the front entrance."

"What are you going to do?"

"There is an old Italian woman here who returned from a trip abroad a few weeks ago. Her room, if I am correct, looks out directly over the street in front of the Lazaretto. She always says that she sits all day and looks out of her window. Perhaps she saw something."

"I hope so."

"So wait outside. I think I can manage to bring her down to the entrance and have you stay right outside to talk to her. She doesn't hear very well and her Italian is a difficult dialect, so I will serve as interpreter."

"Go with *hatzlachah*, Vitorio," I said as I headed out the building.

Outside, I waited, reciting Tehillim. After what seemed

like ages, I saw Vitorio at the Lazaretto's entrance; he waved for me to come over. Behind him, an elderly woman sat in a chair. I stood just outside the doorway, and she sat just inside. Vitorio stood between us.

"Signora Mallisi," he said, "this is my friend Avraham."

She nodded at me. I nodded back.

"From where does he come?"

I could make out her dialect but was happy that Vitorio was there.

"He comes from the holy land."

"The holy land?"

"Yes," I said.

"Very nice."

"Signora, we wanted to know if you saw anything unusual while looking out your window during the last half hour."

"Unusual?"

"A friend of ours has disappeared. He was standing right in front of the Lazaretto, and then something happened to him. We cannot find him."

"Tell me about your friend."

Vitorio described Yaakov.

"I saw him, yes."

My ears perked up.

"Did you see anyone else near him?"

"Yes."

My heart skipped a beat.

"Can you tell us about that?"

"There's not much to tell. I saw the young man you described and he was talking to this one." She pointed at me. "Then this one went to tie his shoe and two men came from behind the young man. One walked very close to him on one side and the other walked very close to him on the other side. They walked to a carriage that waited nearby."

"Is it possible that they were actually holding him tightly by the arms?"

"Yes, that could be."

"Ask her if she can describe them," I said, my heart beating rapidly. This woman had actually seen Yaakov's kidnappers!

"My friend wants to know if the Signora can describe the men."

"I could not see their faces, but I could see that one of the men wore a bright red shirt. You don't see that very much in this country."

A bright red shirt, I thought to myself. That was possibly something to go on but not much in a city the size of Livorno. Besides, how long would he be wearing the shirt?

"Were you able to see anything else?"

"Not really. I was, however, able to hear something you might be interested in."

"Oh?"

"I heard one of the men telling the driver to go to the Lorenca Inn."

"The Lorenca Inn?"

I allowed myself to hope. We had a solid lead.

"Yes. Are you familiar with it?"

"Yes, Signora, I am. Are you sure that is what they said?"

"Listen to me, young man. I may not hear very well, but I don't hear things. If I heard it, I heard it."

"That information may prove very helpful."

"I thought it might."

"Signora, is there anything else you can tell us?"

"No, I'm afraid not. Is your friend in danger?"

"I hope not."

"You look like good boys ... I hope you find him soon."

We thanked her, and then Vitorio went to bring her up to her room. "I'll be back soon, Avraham."

As I waited for him, I wondered if the Lorenca Inn would hold any clues as to Yaakov's whereabouts.

"Should we speak to the police?" I asked Vitorio when he came back.

"We can do that, Avraham, but I doubt they'll do very much without more evidence of wrongdoing."

"Then I should check things out at the Lorenca Inn."

"That definitely sounds like a good idea to me."

"How will I get there?"

"By carriage. I have the money. But don't worry, I'm coming with you."

"Don't you have to work?"

"I'll give up my break tomorrow. Wait a moment while I arrange it with my boss. Meanwhile, see if you can get a carriage."

I was glad that Vitorio was coming along; I felt that a little help could not hurt at this point. Seeing a carriage on the next street, I flagged it down. As it came to a halt in front of me, Vitorio returned.

"Let's go," he said, stepping up into the cab of the carriage. I followed him and closed the carriage door behind me. I had never been in a carriage before and I wished I was less nervous so I could enjoy the experience. We sat down.

"To the Lorenca Inn, driver."

"Yes, sir."

"Well, Avraham, you were trying to get a ride on a Livorno carriage before. Now your wish has come true."

"I'd rather it was under different circumstances."

"I can imagine."

"I really should tell Rebbe Yitzchak about this, but I'm afraid to let this lead go without checking into it as soon as possible."

"You're absolutely right. Whoever grabbed Yaakov thought that no one was looking, but Signora Mallisi had a bird's-eye view. We must look into this right away."

After several minutes, the driver announced, "We're here," bringing the carriage to a stop. Vitorio paid the fare and we got out.

The Lorenca Inn consisted of a main building that housed a dining hall and reading rooms, as well as individual cottages where the inn's customers slept.

"They could easily have brought Yaakov into their cottage unnoticed," I said. Vitorio nodded in agreement.

"Let's look in the main building," he suggested.

We approached the building wondering what we would find. Inside, we saw a large reading room. Several people sat reading or dozing in comfortable chairs. Inn attendants, mostly young men of around my age in black and white uniforms, walked about making themselves busy. I felt Vitorio's hand on my arm, and looked at him. He was pointing to a man sleeping on a sofa at the far side of the room. The man was facing away from us, but he wore a bright red shirt. We gently moved around the room so we could get a better look at him. What I saw made me stop in my tracks; it was the captain of the ship we had traveled on.

Suddenly, my head felt dizzy. The captain! I'd known from the start that he would mean trouble. Was he, too, part of Abu Rash's gang? Vitorio sensed that I recognized the man in the bright red shirt. He motioned for me to follow him out of the building.

Outside, he asked, "You know him?"

"Yes. He's the captain of the ship on which we came over."

"Did you have any trouble from him before?"

"Yes, but *this* is completely unexpected."

"Registered sea men can avoid a stay in the Lazaretto," Vitorio said, "so he may have been here in Livorno since you arrived."

"And he's been waiting to find one of us alone so he could grab him."

"Maybe. I suppose it's also possible that he was away on a short voyage and just returned to Livorno."

"He might have come in on the last ship from Alexandria," I suggested. "The one that brought the Arab fellow who is now staying at the Lazaretto."

"Maybe."

"But what's going on here? Is everybody working for Abu Rash?"

"Abu Rash?"

I realized that Vitorio didn't know the purpose of our journey and had probably never heard of Abu Rash. "Abu Rash is our enemy; there's no time to explain now."

"What's our next move?"

"We have to find out if Yaakov is here."

"Right, but how do we do that?"

"Listen, Vitorio, did you notice the inn attendants in the uniforms?"

"Yes."

"What if we borrow one of those uniforms?"

"And have one of us put it on?"

"We'd look like one of the inn attendants."

"Yes, but —"

"Well, then you or I — whoever had the uniform — could knock on the cottage doors and see if we could be of service ..."

"And as we did that, we'd be looking around for signs of Yaakov?"

"Yes. What do you say?"

"Avraham, I think it's a chancy plan and has little hope of working. Don't you think they'd have him hidden in a back room?"

"So you don't think we should do it?"

"I didn't say that, Avraham."

"What *are* you saying, Vitorio?"

"I say we do it."

"But you said it's a chancy plan and probably won't work."

"Yes," he said, smiling. "But I can't think of anything better."

We re-entered the main building of the inn. In the reading room, the captain still slept. It didn't take long for us to notice that the attendants kept going in and out of a service door to the side. "That's probably where we can get a uniform," said Vitorio. "It's too much of a risk for you to stay in here with the captain around; he might recognize you. Go outside and wait nearby. I'm going in to get a uniform."

"Wait a minute," I said. "Isn't it stealing?"

Vitorio shook his head, saying, "Yaakov may be in grave danger. For *pikuach nefesh*, I think it would be permitted for me to borrow a uniform."

I waited outside behind some trees, looking at the cottages. Was Yaakov in one of them? I wondered how this would end. Was Yaakov safe? Was my father safe? What about my mother and sisters? I don't know why all these questions popped into mind just then. Luckily, just then I saw Vitorio coming toward me looking like an inn attendant. The fit was not perfect; the uniform seemed a bit tight, but it would definitely do. He was smiling.

"How did you do that so fast?"

"I just walked in that service entrance, saw an open closet with uniforms, took one and slipped it on. Couldn't have been much easier."

"No one saw you?"

"They did, but they must have thought I was an attendant."

I looked at him seriously. "All right, you did the first part. Now let me have the uniform and I'll go to the cottages."

He shook his head.

"Come on, now," I protested. "I can't let you do everything."

"We can both go to the cottages."

"How?"

He smiled and removed the uniform. Beneath it, he had on another uniform. "After I put on one uniform, I figured I might as well get a second one for you."

I laughed. "I thought it didn't fit you. Little did I know you had on another uniform."

"You thought it didn't fit? Are you saying I'm overweight?"

I laughed again. It was good to be able to laugh, even when I felt so worried. I offered a silent prayer to Hashem that we would soon have good reason to laugh.

"We'll both go," said Vitorio, turning serious, "but you'll have to be especially cautious, in case that captain comes around."

I nodded in agreement and donned my uniform.

We agreed that I would take the cottages on the right side of the inn, while Vitorio would take those on the left.

Right after Vitorio left for his side of the inn, I began to wonder if people would find it strange that the attendant coming to ask if he could be of service was barely able to speak Italian. I noticed Vitorio was already knocking on a cottage door. Then I remembered that I'd heard one of the attendants in the main building speaking with a heavy accent of some sort. I hoped he was not the exception. It was very likely that many of the visitors staying at the inn were from out of the country, so it might not be so strange to hear an attendant who knew as little of the language as they did. I tried to convince myself that this was in fact the case as I approached the first cottage door.

Offering a quick *tefillah*, I knocked. As I waited to see if there would be any answer, I looked back over my shoulder to make sure that the captain was nowhere in sight. I waited a minute and then knocked again. No answer.

I went to the next cottage and knocked on the door. Again there was no response. There was, however, someone in the third cottage. A sleepy looking man asked me what I wanted.

"The inn would like to know if you need anything," I said.

"No," he said and slammed the door. I had not even been able to see past him. For all I knew, Yaakov could be in there. Vitorio was right; this really was a silly plan. I went to the next cottage, where there was no answer. At the next one, a woman asked if she could order a cannoli.

"I don't know," I said, "but I can check."

"Oh, just forget about it. I don't understand. You asked me if I want anything. I want a cannoli, but you don't even know if you have. Why do you ask, then?"

I shrugged, feeling a little guilty, and went on to the next cottage. There was no answer. I was getting discouraged and wondered if Vitorio was doing any better, when I knocked on cottage 5B. A tall man who didn't look like he smiled much answered the door. "What is it?"

"The inn would like to know if you need anything."

"I've been here before, and this is the first time an attendant has come around to the cottages."

"That's right," I said. "We just started."

"Like what?"

"What do you mean?"

"You asked me if I need anything. What would I need? Give me an example."

"Well, one woman wanted a cannoli, for example."

"A cannoli. Why? Can you can bring me a cannoli?"

I regretted my stupidity. "I can check ...."

He looked at me. "Listen, if I want anything, I'll come to the main building, all right?"

"Yes," I said. Then I heard someone saying a few words of

Ashrei. It was Yaakov's voice, I was sure of it. He was probably davening Minchah. He was in this cottage! The man looked closely at me to see if I'd heard, but I tried my best not to let him know I had.

"Tell them not to send anyone here again, all right?"

"Yes, sir."

He slammed the door, and I went to get Vitorio, my heart pounding. We'd found Yaakov!

CHAPTER FIFTEEN

I found Vitorio as he was about to knock on another door.

"I've found him!"

"What?"

"I know where Yaakov is being held."

"Where?"

"Cottage 5B."

"How do you know?"

I told him what I'd overheard, and we started to walk away from the cottages. Just then a nearby door opened, and an old man stood in the doorway.

"Kid, I changed my mind," he said. "I want you to get me something."

"Sorry, sir," said Vitorio. "Our shift just finished, and the next attendant will take your order."

We left the man standing there. Removing our uniforms, we left them near the service entrance and then walked a short distance away.

"You're sure it was him?"

"Yes. I'm going to get Rebbe Yitzchak right now," I said. "You must stay here to watch in case they try to take Yaakov somewhere else."

"Good idea, Avraham. Do you have the carriage fare to get to the Pereira home?"

"Yes."

"Hurry back. There's no telling when they could try to move Yaakov."

"I will," I said as I ran toward an approaching carriage. The carriage ride seemed to take forever, but of course it was only my impatience and worry for Yaakov that made it seem that way. When we arrived at the Pereira home, I paid the fare and jumped off.

In the house I found Signor Michael Pereira himself sitting in the front salon.

"Signor, is Rebbe Yitzchak here?"

"No, he's out, Avraham."

"It's very important for me to see him as soon as possible. Do you know where he went?"

"I do. He was planning to go first to the telegraph office and then to the old Jewish cemetery to visit the *kever* of Rebbe Chaim Cohen, who is buried here in Livorno. He was a *talmid* of Rebbe Chaim Vital."

"When did he leave?"

"About ten minutes ago."

"Do you think I could still get him at the telegraph office?"

"I'm afraid I couldn't say. It depends on the type of business he had there."

It's funny how even in times of stress, undisciplined thoughts can make their way into your mind. When Signor Pereira said this, I thought to myself, *And why is Rebbe Yitzchak so busy with the telegraph office in every city we visit?* It's strange how the mind works.

"Is it far from here?"

"Not very. Neither is the cemetery."

"I appreciate your time, Signor. I must be going."

"You'll be able to get a carriage right in front."

"Yes, thank you. By the way, would you happen to know if Ahmed is here?"

"I believe he is."

I decided to run upstairs and get Ahmed. Perhaps he would be of use. With Ahmed following, I ran out of the house and hailed the first carriage to drive by.

"Where to?" the driver asked.

"The telegraph office."

"Yes, Signor."

At the telegraph office, Rebbe Yitzchak was nowhere to be found. I'd told the driver to wait for us, and we climbed back on the carriage.

"To the old Jewish cemetery," I instructed the driver.

I wondered how this would end as the carriage sped down the streets. When we started this journey, I'd looked forward to the adventure, but things were getting a little too adventurous for me. As usual, I was angry with myself for being afraid, but that didn't change my feelings.

My thoughts were interrupted when the carriage stopped.

"We're here, sir."

Ahmed waited outside the gate. I went inside the cemetery, walking on a path between rows of old graves. Not far ahead I saw Rebbe Yitzchak. The sight of him calmed me. He stood straight as a rod, his eyes closed. Tears ran down his cheeks onto his beard. I didn't know if I should interrupt him. Time was of the essence, so I decided that I would have to speak up. Just then, Rebbe Yitzchak opened his eyes. He turned and saw me.

"Avraham, we are not *mispallel* to the *neshamos*, of course. We only take advantage of their merits."

I nodded.

"Rebbe Chaim Cohen was a student of Rebbe Chaim Vital, who was the prime student of the holy Ari," he said, pointing at the *kever*.

"Yes, Rebbe."

"What brings you here, Avraham?"

I quickly filled in Rebbe Yitzchak on Yaakov's disappearance and how we had found him as well as our captain. As he listened, his face became grave. When I finished my account, he said, "We must go to the inn immediately."

"I have a carriage waiting."

"Good."

"I brought Ahmed along. He may be helpful."

Rebbe Yitzchak said, "If you wish," but his expression seemed to imply, *Ahmed or no Ahmed, Yaakov is coming home with us.* At that moment, I was sure glad I was on Rebbe Yitzchak's side. As soon as we got in the carriage, Rebbe Yitzchak said, "To the Lorenca Inn, driver — quickly, please."

"Yes, sir."

When we arrived at the inn, we found Vitorio pacing nervously. Rebbe Yitzchak shook his hand warmly. "You must be Vitorio. Avraham has told me about you. Tell me, what has happened since Avraham left to get me?"

"The captain came out of the main building and went into the cottage."

"No one left the cottage?"

"No, Rebbe."

"Please show me to the cottage."

We brought Rebbe Yitzchak to cottage 5B. He went to the door and knocked. As we waited for an answer, he looked at Vitorio and myself and said, "Remember, there is only One true Power; there is no other."

The door opened and our friend the captain stood there in his red shirt, his huge eyes glaring at us. There was a flicker of surprise in those big frightening eyes, but it soon vanished and was replaced with a look of impatience.

"Rabbi," he said tersely, "I didn't think I would see you here."

"Is that so?"

"What brings you here, Rabbi?"

Rebbe Yitzchak ignored him and called into the cottage, "Yaakov, you will be with us shortly. Have no fear."

The captain stepped out of the cottage and closed the door behind him. "What do you want?"

"The boy. Let him out now."

"You must remember that he destroyed a barrel of oil on my ship."

"What has that to do with us now?"

"He has to repay the damages. You are an ethical man.

You understand that one must pay one's debts. That is why he is here. He is working for me until his bill is paid."

I almost laughed out loud. So our captain was not part of the Abu Rash gang after all. He was just greedy.

"He worked on the ship," said Rebbe Yitzchak. "That, I believe, paid off his debt. Your holding him now is unlawful."

"I say his debt is not repaid."

"I'm sorry to say, you are wrong."

The captain's face turned red. "He'll stay until I say his debt is repaid!"

"He will come with us now," Rebbe Yitzchak declared with absolute calm.

"And if I choose not to let him go?"

"You have little choice in the matter, captain."

"Oh?" said the captain.

"Should I call the authorities now? You don't want to waste your time in an Italian jail for the crime of kidnapping, do you, captain?"

"I'll bring witnesses from the ship that he did damage. It will be impossible to prove that he fully repaid the debt."

"That is an excuse for abducting him?"

"Listen, Rabbi, I have friends here in Livorno in the court system. They will see this as a case of a hardworking fellow simply trying to make up his damages."

"I see. Tell me, captain, how is business on your ship?"

The captain's large eyes narrowed. "What do you mean by that?"

"I mean that the company that employs you depends on you to maintain their reputation."

"What are you driving at?"

"If on your watch, the ship was found to be unfit, it would affect business for your employers. It might even cause trouble with the Italian authorities."

"What are you saying? I keep a perfect ship."

"The Italian authorities seem to be quite sensitive to foreigners coming here and bringing various diseases. That's why they have the Lazaretto."

"You are talking in riddles, Rabbi."

"I have a feeling that it is not widely known that you brought a ship into the port of Livorno that was heavily infested with worms."

The captain's large eyes opened fully. He was about to say something, but didn't.

"I have several witnesses to the extent of that infestation. I'm sure the port officials will be very interested in my story."

The captain said nothing, but there was a look of panic in his eyes.

"I keep a perfect ship," he said weakly.

"Tell that to the worms that were feasting on my provisions."

Rebbe Yitzchak walked past the captain and into the cottage. As he did so, he said, "Perhaps the authorities would also be interested in hearing about the chest that fell on a passenger's bed — the chest that would likely have caused grievous injury had anyone been unfortunate enough to have been in that bed at the time."

The captain stood silent.

A moment later, Rebbe Yitzchak came out of the cottage leading Yaakov by the hand, and I thought of his words on the ship: *"Apparently the worms carried out their mission well. Let us hope that we carry out our missions as well as they did."*

(

Yaakov was, *baruch Hashem*, fine — a bit shaken perhaps, but otherwise fine.

When we had a chance to speak later, Yaakov said, "Avraham, as I told you before, it seems that the expression 'like father, like son' really applies to me. My father was taken away by a scoundrel to work off his debt, and that seems to be my fate as well."

"Come on, Yaakov, don't say that. No one is taking you anywhere. Not if Rebbe Yitzchak has anything to say about it."

Yaakov smiled. "That's true."

For a moment there was silence and then Yaakov said, "Speaking of Rebbe Yitzchak, there's something I never got a chance to ask you because … well, I guess because at the time we weren't on such good speaking terms. Remember when we were stopped by Abu Rash? Somehow we got past him. Can you explain to me what happened there?"

"Rebbe Yitzchak once told me that some things we don't talk about."

"Oh, so you know but won't talk about it?"

I laughed. "I didn't say that. I'm just telling you what Rebbe Yitzchak once told me. Apparently, these things happen rarely and only under certain extreme circumstances. More than that, I don't know."

"He's amazing."

"Yaakov, I'll tell you something my father once told me

about Rebbe Yitzchak. He said that the really amazing thing about him is his extraordinary diligence in the study of Torah, his unusual *yiras Shamayim* and his unparalleled concern for others. These, he said, are his real miracles."

As I related my father's words to Yaakov, a powerful sadness gripped me. I missed my father terribly, and I hated not knowing where he was or what was happening to him. My voice began to quiver a little and I might actually have started to tear up, but then I thought of Yaakov and controlled myself. It's not that I was ashamed to show him my sadness. It was the fact that at least I had every reason to believe that my father was alive and that I would see him again. Yaakov did not have that luxury.

Yaakov was apparently also busy thinking. After a minute, he said, "Yes. I also think that Rebbe Yitzchak would say that everything is really a miracle. Some miracles might be open, but most are just hidden in nature."

"Yes, I think you're right; that's exactly what he would say. I think that's what he means when he says that Hashem is One —"

"There is no other," said Yaakov, finishing my sentence.

"Exactly," I said. "He means that you can really see Hashem's hand in everything."

"If you look for it," Yaakov added.

"Yes."

We had been talking in front of the Pereira home and now looked up to see a carriage stop in front of us. Rebbe Yitzchak stepped down; he had been to the telegraph office again.

"Yaakov, Avraham, start packing your things and tell

Ahmed to do the same," he said. "We will be leaving Livorno tomorrow."

"Where are we headed, Rebbe?" I asked.

"Germany."

"Do we have any idea where we will be going from Germany?"

"Very possibly Holland."

We went to pack, and Ahmed helped. While we were packing, Yaakov asked me something that was bothering him.

"Why is Rebbe Yitzchak traveling from country to country, Avraham? Germany, Holland — there must be some reason."

"Well, you know the reason I'm here is to stay out of the hands of Abu Rash."

"Although his people seem to be on our trail," Yaakov added.

"Perhaps Rebbe Yitzchak is trying to outrun them."

"Maybe."

"Also, he's traveling a route that he uses on his missions for Eretz Yisrael. He figures that he may as well do some fundraising once we're in Europe anyway."

"Everything you say sounds right, but I think there's more to it."

"Well, you told me that Rebbe Yitzchak plans to go to Izmir, Turkey, to find your father's grave."

"Yes, but there's something else determining where we go and when we leave a certain place, and it has to do with all the telegraphing Rebbe Yitzchak does."

"You have a point there."

"Well, maybe one day, we'll figure it out."

"Maybe, Yaakov."

We continued packing in silence until I said, "You know, Yaakov, something has been bothering me for a while, and I wonder what you think about it."

"Let's hear."

"We have to do for others, right?"

"Of course."

"But a person has to do for himself also, don't you think?"

"Well … yes. I mean, someone else can't learn a *daf Gemara* for you."

I laughed. "Exactly."

"So what's the problem?"

"What I want to know is, which is the most important thing? What should be the main focus, our own growth or the success of others?"

Yaakov thought for a moment and then said, "You know, it just hit me that your question is actually mentioned in a *mishnah* in Avos where it says, 'If I am not for myself, then who will be? And if I am for myself, then what am I?'"

I laughed. "Yaakov, you're right! That *mishnah* slipped my mind, but that's probably what the *mishnah* is talking about."

"But that doesn't really answer your question."

"True," I said. "The *mishnah* raises the question, but doesn't seem to answer it."

"Maybe we can ask Rebbe Yitzchak."

"Sounds like a good idea to me," I said.

Suddenly, we were interrupted by a knock on the door of our room.

"Come in," I said.

A servant entered the room. "You have a guest waiting downstairs."

Yaakov looked at me. "A guest?"

I shrugged. "Let's go and see."

Promising each other to continue this conversation another time, we headed for the stairs.

CHAPTER SIXTEEN

ownstairs, we found Vitorio standing in the front salon.

"Vitorio, what brings you here?" I asked, happy to see our new friend.

"Your Arab friend from the Lazaretto brings me here, Avraham."

"What do you mean?"

"I'll tell you in a moment, but first let me ask you something, Avraham."

"Go ahead," I said.

"This Abu Rash who is causing you fellows all this grief ..."

"Yes?"

"Would it make sense that he would be after other members of your family as well?"

I wondered what Vitorio was driving at but said, "Yes, Vitorio, that definitely sounds right."

Vitorio looked at me for a moment and then said, "Avraham, maybe you'll think I've lost my senses, but I have to ask —"

"Go ahead, Vitorio!" I exclaimed, wondering what he could possibly be getting at.

"Avraham, do you have a brother by the name of Zerachia?"

I don't know what I'd been expecting Vitorio to say, but I certainly had not been expecting this. "Zerachia? I haven't spoken to him in over a year. How do you know about Zerachia?"

"So he's your brother?"

"We consider him our brother, yes. But Vitorio, tell me what's going on here."

"It's a long story, but I'll make it short," said Vitorio. "For several years, I've been carrying on a correspondence with students of a certain yeshivah in Eastern Europe renowned for its young scholars. Not having an abundance of like-minded people my age to converse with about my studies and the like, I felt that keeping in touch by pen would be a good way of having contact with students in the great yeshivos of the world. Anyway, there is one student in the yeshivah I mentioned in Europe —"

"Which yeshivah?" Yaakov asked.

"I can't really say, as the fellow made me promise not to divulge his location to anyone."

"All right, go on, then," I said.

"As I was saying, there is one student in this yeshivah

with whom I have developed a regular correspondence. We discuss what we are studying, but we also discuss things that are happening in our lives. Now, the other day when you mentioned the name Abu Rash, I had never heard of the man. I gathered that he was causing you a world of trouble, but other than that, I knew nothing of him.

"This morning, a letter arrived at my home by post from the student I am corresponding with. In it, he tells me about this criminal leader by the name of Abu Rash who is gaining power in Eretz Yisrael. When I saw that name, I almost fell off my chair, as that was the name you had mentioned.

"He then related that apparently this Abu Rash must be after him and his family for some reason since he'd been told that members of his gang have been trying to find him in Europe. Their spies had even reached Eastern Europe, and he's now trying to stay in hiding until this passes. He wanted me to know that my letters might not reach him at the old address for a while, and that's why he was writing now. He gave no new address.

"He also tells me that he is worried about his family back in Eretz Yisrael — his father, his mother, his sisters … and his brother Avraham."

"You were corresponding with Zerachia!" I exclaimed.

"Yes, the name of the fellow I correspond with is Zerachia. I may not be the brightest fellow in Livorno, but when I saw that he was also in trouble with a man named Abu Rash and that he had a brother in Eretz Yisrael named Avraham, I said to myself, 'Vitorio, my boy, believe it or not, I think you have been corresponding with Avraham's brother all these months.'"

I didn't know what to say at first. The first thing that struck me was that Zerachia had referred to me as his brother in a letter to someone whom he had no idea knew me. He hadn't called me an adopted brother or ... whatever he might have called me; he just called me his brother. I was really touched by that.

The next thing I thought was, *So that's where he's been all this time*! Although I still didn't know exactly where he was, at least I had some idea. I'd had a feeling he was out of Eretz Yisrael but I'd always been curious as to where he'd gone. Now I knew. He'd gone to study in one of the great European yeshivos. The truth is, it didn't really surprise me; that's just the type of thing he would do.

The last thought that struck me was fear. They were all over, these cursed men! Did they have to track down even Zerachia? What did they want from him? Was being part of our family such a crime? I wondered if my mother and sisters would in fact be safe in Eretz Yisrael. These people seemed to be willing to stop at nothing. Then I thought about what Rebbe Yitzchak would say if I'd voice these concerns to him, and I calmed down a bit.

I paused for a moment simply to digest all of these thoughts. Then, not knowing what else to do, I smiled. "Vitorio, I think you're right. It turns out you knew my brother before you knew me."

"Quite so," he said with a smile.

"Amazing, isn't it?" Yaakov asked.

"It is definitely amazing," I agreed. Then, turning to Vitorio, I asked, "Did it sound like he was in actual danger, Vitorio?"

"No, Avraham, not imminent danger, but his *rosh yeshivah* felt that it would be prudent to take precautions immediately."

"I'll repeat what I've told you before, Avraham," Yaakov said. "I am not a great admirer of Abu Rash, to say the least."

Vitorio smiled. "Yaakov, from the little I know of this gentleman, no decent person would admire him."

We were all silent for a moment until I said, "But Vitorio, this is not the real reason for your visit, is it?"

"No, I'm actually here to tell you something about your Arab friend from the Lazaretto."

"And that is ...?" Yaakov said curiously.

"He's gone."

Yaakov waved his hand nervously. "What does that mean?"

"He left the Lazaretto about an hour ago."

"He snuck out?" I asked.

"No. He apparently was allowed to leave."

"But doesn't he have to stay for another few weeks?" Yaakov asked.

"We knew he had some type of influence when we saw him talking to the other Arab fellow. Well, apparently he has even more influence than we thought."

"The people at the Lazaretto were influenced by some of Abu Rash's money," I muttered angrily.

"It's very possible, Avraham. One thing is certain, though; he's no longer in the Lazaretto. I wanted to come as soon as I could, to let you know that he was on the loose together with his friend."

"We very much appreciate that, young man," came a familiar voice.

We all turned to see Rebbe Yitzchak coming down the stairs.

"Although we will be leaving your fine city tomorrow, it is useful to know that he is free to move around as he pleases. After all, they have been quite adept at following us."

"Then this will be a good opportunity for me to wish Rebbe and you two fellows '*tzeischem leshalom.*'"

We wished Vitorio well and promised to somehow stay in touch with him. Then Rebbe Yitzchak took him aside. They spoke for several minutes. Rebbe Yitzchak pointed to a pile of papers and a quill and ink that stood on the salon table for use by whoever needed it. Vitorio wrote for about a minute, and then we said our final good-byes and he left.

"I suggest you fellows finish packing, do some learning, have something to eat and then go to bed. We have some traveling coming up."

We readily followed Rebbe Yitzchak's advice.

The next morning, we loaded our things on to a large carriage. When the driver asked if we were ready to go, Rebbe Yitzchak said we were. Signor Michael Pereira stood with his entire family and staff of household help to give Rebbe Yitzchak a proper send-off. As the carriage started down the street, Rebbe Yitzchak waved out the window. Signor Pereira waved solemnly. He was so overcome with emotion over Rebbe Yitzchak's departure that tears actually welled up in his eyes.

"You will be blessed in many ways, Signor Michael," Rebbe Yitzchak called.

I looked back for as long as I could see them. No one

moved. The entire group stood still. I imagine they stood that way until they could no longer see our carriage. Is there another people that honors the Torah as we do?

CHAPTER SEVENTEEN

We traveled by carriage from city to city in Italy, generally staying in a place for only one night, unless it was the end of the week, in which case we would stay for the entire Shabbos. Generally, noted members of the local Jewish community graciously gave us food and lodging.

When we were in Padua, the city in which Rebbe Moshe Chaim Luzzato had lived, Rebbe Yitzchak wanted to visit the city of Venice to see certain manuscripts there. We traveled by boat from Padua to Venice, where we found lodging in a room in the back of a *beis kenesses*.

While Rebbe Yitzchak was out searching for his manuscripts, Yaakov and I decided to have a look around Venice. I, of course, knew something about the famous city, thanks to Uncle Gavriel. When Yaakov asked for information about the city, I told him that although we were in the part of the city that was on the Italian mainland, much of the city was actually built on about a hundred and twenty islands. A lagoon separates the islands of Venice from the mainland and a causeway connects the mainland to two of the islands.

Yaakov wanted to get over that causeway and onto the islands, and so did I. We headed that way, and I told him that when Venice had been an independent empire, it was such a strong sea power that it was known as the "Queen of the Adriatic," as it was located off the northeast coast of Italy at the north end of the Adriatic Sea.

In the 1400s, when Christopher Columbus had sailed to America and Vasco de Gama had found a sea route to India, the center of trade had shifted to the Atlantic Ocean, and Venice's power had declined. Its eastern colonies were eventually lost to the Ottoman Empire. In 1797, the French forces of Napoleon Bonaparte had occupied Venice. What remained of the empire was divided between France and Austria, with the city of Venice itself under Austrian control. I told Yaakov that right now, as we spoke, it was being decided if Venice would become part of the independent Kingdom of Italy.

We finally found our way across the causeway and saw that the city was as beautiful as Uncle Gavriel had said it was. Instead of streets, more than one hundred and fifty canals are used to get around. Black flat-bottomed boats known as gondolas are the main form of transportation around the islands. The gondolas are guided along the canals by men known as gondoliers. There are also many bridges that link the main islands of the city. Narrow alleyways called *calli* run between the buildings on the islands. Just moving around the city was fascinating, and Yaakov and I spent hours looking around.

The Rialto Bridge crosses the Grand Canal, which winds through the heart of the city. Amazing marble and stone palaces that were built between the 1100s and the 1800s line both sides of the Grand Canal. I had also heard about the famous Bridge of Sighs that crosses the canal. The bridge had been designed by Italian architect Antonio Contino and was completed in 1602. It got its name from the sad prisoners who used to pass through a passageway on the bridge on their way from prison to the palace for trial. Those who were found guilty were sent to execution through another passageway of the bridge. When we finally found this bridge, Yaakov exclaimed, "Avraham, I would never have believed that touring a city could be so interesting."

Venice doesn't have many parks or gardens, so we took note when after hours of touring we came to a little public garden filled with brilliantly colored flowers.

"Nice, no?" Yaakov remarked.

I nodded in agreement.

"I wouldn't mind sitting on that bench under the tree for a while."

"What are you, an old lady?" I teased.

"Why? Do I have to be an old lady to want to sit for a minute?"

"All right, then, an old man."

"Avraham, I'm surprised at you. I'm sure Rebbe Yitzchak would be in favor of taking a minute to appreciate this wonderful example of Hashem's creation. Besides, I don't know about you, but I personally am a bit tired from all this traveling and the exploring we've done today."

"I'm just joking, Yaakov. If you want to sit, we'll sit. Anything for a friend in need."

"In need? I'm just a little tired."

"Stop being so sensitive, Yaakov. You know I'm joking."

We sat down, and I have to admit that the scene was really beautiful.

"Yaakov, do you think Rebbe Yitzchak found the manuscripts he was looking for?"

"If they were here, I'm sure he found them."

I smiled. Yaakov was right. If Rebbe Yitzchak came all the way here for something, he probably wouldn't give up until he found it. I thought for a moment and then spoke.

"I've been wondering about that *sefer* Rebbe Yitzchak wrote in the Lazaretto. Are you sure you heard him say that he wrote it on my account?"

"I think so."

"What could he have meant by that?"

"I really don't know, Avraham."

"Maybe he was talking about a different Avraham."

"It could be. I'm not sure why I assumed he meant you, but somehow I still think he did."

"Yaakov, can I ask you something?"

"Yes, sure."

"Do you think someone can have fears and still be a *baal bitachon*?"

"You mean that if he truly believed, he wouldn't be afraid?"

"Right."

"I guess you might be right, but I don't know if it's either one or the other."

"What do you mean?"

"I mean, it's true that someone with perfect *emunah* and *bitachon* might not really have many fears, but none of us are perfect. So if you ask me if it's a contradiction when one person has *bitachon* at some times, and is fearful at others, I'd say no. That person is working on his belief. Sometimes he's able to reach a level of faith that calms him, and other times he isn't. Does that mean that the times he had faith weren't real? I don't think so."

"I see what you mean. One day a person might do something really good, and yet in that same day he might trip up and do something not so great. As you said, does that mean that when he did good, it wasn't sincere? No. It just means that at one point he was able to do good and at another he wasn't."

"You're saying that this doesn't only apply to faith but to any test we have. Sometimes we pass and sometimes we don't."

"Yes. I mean that Hashem gives us free will. Sometimes we choose the right thing, but when we don't, it doesn't mean that when we did, we weren't sincere."

Yaakov laughed. "And it's a good thing, because if that's the way things worked, we'd never get anywhere. Because as you say, we always have free will, and if every time we fail, we lose everything we've accomplished, very few people would be left with anything."

We sat in silence until Yaakov called my attention to something rather disturbing.

"Avraham, does that remind you of home?"

"What are you talking about?"

"Look over there."

I turned in the direction he was pointing and saw a group of Greek Orthodox priests in their long black robes and caps, their long beards waving gently in the breeze.

"Home?"

"Well, you see them in Yerushalayim, don't you?"

"I don't know if I would quite call that a reminder of home."

"You don't think these are the priests who were involved in taking the boy from Yerushalayim, do you?"

"I wonder, Yaakov. The church here is Catholic — not Greek Orthodox — so these fellows are probably visitors from somewhere else."

"The question is, why are they here?"

We sat watching the men, who seemed to be waiting for something or someone for several minutes. Then another black-clad priest came over to the group and they all started to walk. We were now able to see them from a slightly different angle.

We saw him at the same time.

"Avraham, do you see who I see?"

"Yes, Yaakov, I do. I don't believe what I'm seeing, but I do see it."

He was dressed in the garb of a Greek Orthodox priest, but it was him, I was sure of it. So was Yaakov, who'd seen him as he left Rebbe Chaim Provencal's house.

There among the group of bearded priests walked Rebbe Yekusiel of Tzefas.

C

We got back to our room before Rebbe Yitzchak did. As we prepared ourselves something to eat, Yaakov repeated a question he had asked me on our way back.

"Avraham, could you explain to me what Rebbe Yekusiel was doing walking with those priests?"

I smiled. "My answer to you now is the same as the last time you asked me this question. I have no idea."

"He wasn't just walking with them, he was dressed like them. Can you explain that?"

Laughing, I said, "You already asked that as well, and my answer is still the same. I haven't any explanation."

"I don't understand this. You don't find this strange?"

"Why do you think I don't find it strange? I find it extremely strange and frankly, somewhat scary. I just have no explanation for it."

"I mean, if I hadn't seen him before, I would never have realized he wasn't one of those priests. He blended in so well."

"You're right. I mean, once I looked it was clear to me who he was, but if I'd just been passing by and had never seen him, I wouldn't have noticed."

Without any answers, we turned to our meal of bread and cheese.

"I've noticed that this business of walking around cities can really make you hungry," Yaakov said as he brought water for us to wash our hands.

"I think I've noticed that as well."

We'd just finished saying Birkas Hamazon when Rebbe Yitzchak returned.

"Can I make Rebbe something to eat?"

"No, Yaakov. I appreciate the offer, but I had something before I left."

"Was Rebbe successful?"

"Yes, *baruch Hashem*, Avraham. I found the manuscript I was looking for."

Yaakov and I exchanged knowing glances.

"I spent most of the day copying passages that I needed. I hope you were not bored here."

We laughed and told Rebbe Yitzchak of our adventures, ending with our disturbing sighting of Rebbe Yekusiel of Tzefas among the priests.

Rebbe Yitzchak was silent for a moment. "Interesting," he finally said. "Did he see you?"

"I don't think so," I answered.

"No, he gave no sign of having noticed us," Yaakov added.

"Rebbe, what could it mean?" I asked. "He's the one who told us that Abu Rash had something personal against my family. Can we trust him?"

"I don't know, but everyone has their own mission. Perhaps he is on a mission we do not yet fully understand."

The words Rebbe Yekusiel had spoken to us in Alexandria came back to me: *As you, Rebbe Yitzchak, know better than most, everyone has their own mission.* I wondered what type of mission Rebbe Yekusiel was on. Was he really who he said he was?

Two days later we made the trip back to Padua, part of the way by gondola and part of the way by carriage.

As we sat in the gondola, Yaakov pointed to another gondola a distance away. Sitting inside was the Arab who had chased me into the mosque in Alexandria and then followed us to Livorno.

"He's everywhere!" I said in frustration.

"Not everywhere, believe me," Rebbe Yitzchak said with complete calm.

"When will they leave us alone?" I fretted.

"Pay him no attention," Rebbe Yitzchak said as if he were talking of a fly. "They can do nothing to us here."

I did not know exactly what Rebbe Yitzchak meant by that. But, whatever he meant, it certainly made me feel better.

When we arrived back in Padua, Rebbe Yitzchak insisted on taking us to see a garden maze where the plants are arranged to form various confusing and interlacing paths. The idea was to challenge the visitor to reach the structure in the middle.

"The Ramchal, who lived in this very city, uses such a maze to illustrate a very important lesson," Rebbe Yitzchak told us as we looked at the imposing maze.

"He writes that one who walks through the maze has no way of seeing or knowing whether he is on the true or false path. But one who stands high up in the center structure sees all the paths before him and can see which are true and lead to the center, and which are false and lead nowhere.

"So, too, writes the Ramchal, one who has not yet conquered his *yetzer hara* is like one who is in the midst of the paths and cannot distinguish between them. But those who have conquered their *yetzer hara* are like those who have reached the center structure and can clearly see all the paths. They can advise one who is on the paths, if he is willing to listen.

"Here, boys, you see exactly what the Ramchal was talking about. The holy Chida in his travel diary, when he speaks of his visit to Padua, tells of seeing just such a garden maze."

The maze was pretty interesting, and the message it symbolized was inspiring, but to me the most touching thing about the visit was the eagerness with which Rebbe Yitzchak described it. His eyes shone like those of a youngster as he spoke. I will remember those few words that he spoke to us near the maze in Padua for a long time.

☾

It was getting dark and we headed back to where we were staying.

That night I dreamed of Rebbe Yekusiel. He was dressed as a priest. We were in a long dark maze, and he was walking toward me.

"Who are you?" I asked.

"Don't be afraid of me, Avraham," he said.

"Then who should I be afraid of?"

He pointed behind me.

I turned and saw the man without a face, the man with darkness for a face.

I froze in terror. "Help!" I screamed.

"What is it?" Yaakov asked.

I opened my eyes.

"Is everything all right, Avraham?"

I smiled weakly. "Don't tell me you were awake this time too."

"No. This time you woke me up."

"I'm really sorry."

"There's no reason to be sorry. What was it?" Yaakov asked. "Rebbe Yekusiel or the darkness fellow?"

I laughed. "Both."

"Both? You certainly have complicated dreams."

"How did you know what I dreamed about, Yaakov?"

He waved his hand impatiently.

"Tell me, Yaakov, how did you know I was dreaming of Rebbe Yekusiel?"

"I just knew."

"How did you know?"

He hesitated for a moment and then he said, "Because I also dreamed of him."

The next morning, we continued on. Several days later, shortly before nightfall, we arrived in the city of Innsbruck. After several weeks of travel, we had arrived in Germany.

CHAPTER EIGHTEEN

We moved quickly from one town to another, much as we had done in Italy after leaving Livorno, and in less than two weeks we were in the city of Hanau. The night we spent there, something strange happened.

We slept at the home of a local Jewish businessman named Reb Wolf Landau. Rebbe Yitzchak slept in one room, while Yaakov and I slept in another. Ahmed slept in a room that, although separate from ours, was adjoining it. At one point in the middle of the night, Yaakov woke me.

"What is it?" I asked.

"Listen."

From the adjoining room I could hear a man's voice. The man was speaking Arabic. I couldn't really hear what he was